Prayers That Avail Much

James 5:16

by
Word Ministries, Inc.

Revised Edition 1980

And this is the confidence that we have in him, that, if we ask any thing according to his will, he heareth us: and if we know that he hear us, whatsoever we ask, we know that we have the petitions that we desired of him.

1 John 5:14,15

HARRISON HOUSE
Tulsa, Oklahoma

11th Printing
Over 415,000 in Print

Prayers That Avail Much
ISBN 0-89274-116-3
Copyright © 1980 by Word Ministries, Inc.
P. O. Box 76532
Atlanta, Georgia 30358

Published by Harrison House, Inc.
P. O. Box 35035
Tulsa, Oklahoma 74153

DEDICATION

This book is dedicated to our Lord and Savior Jesus Christ.

"The Lord gave the Word: great was the company of those that published it" (Psalm 68:11).

Special thanks to Jan Duncan, Carolyn East, Pat Gastineau, Frankie Patterson, Barbara Patton, and Pat Porter for their share in this book.

Germaine Copeland, President
Word Ministries, Inc.

Table of Contents

Fellowship:

General:

Health:

Home:

Finances:

Foreword

The prayers in this book are to be used by you for yourself and for others. They are a matter of the heart. On purpose feed them into your spirit. Allow the Holy Spirit to make the Word a reality in your heart. Your spirit will become quickened to God's Word, and you will begin to think like God thinks and talk like He talks. You will find yourself poring over His Word — hungering for more and more. The Father rewards those who diligently seek Him. (Hebrews 11:6.)

Meditate upon the scriptures listed with these prayers. These are by no means the only scriptures on certain subjects, but they are a beginning.

These prayers are to be a help and a guide to you in order for you to get better acquainted with your heavenly Father and His Word. Not only does His Word affect your life, but also it will affect others through you, for you will be able to counsel accurately those who come to you for advice. If you can't counsel someone with the Word, you don't have anything with which to counsel. Walk in God's counsel, and prize His wisdom. (Psalm 1; Proverbs 4:7-8.) People are looking for something on which they can depend. When someone in need comes to you, you can point him to that portion in God's Word that is the answer to his problem. You become victorious, trustworthy, and the one with the answer, for your heart is fixed and established on His Word. (Psalm 112.)

Once you begin delving into God's Word, you must commit to ordering your conversation aright. (Psalm 50:23.) That's being a doer of the Word. Faith always has a good report. You can't pray effectively for yourself, for someone, or about something and then talk negatively about the matter. (Matthew 12:34-37.)

This is being double minded, and a double minded man receives *nothing* from God. (James 1:6-8.)

In Ephesians 4:29-30 it is written, *"Let no foul or polluting language, nor evil word, nor unwholesome or worthless talk (ever) come out of your mouth; but only such (speech) as is good and beneficial to the spiritual progress of others, as is fitting to the need and the occasion, that it may be a blessing and give grace (God's favor) to those who hear it. And do not grieve the Holy Spirit of God, (do not offend, or vex, or sadden Him) by whom you were sealed (marked, branded as God's own, secured) for the day of redemption — of final deliverance through Christ from evil and the consequences of sin"* (Amplified).

Allow those words to sink into your innermost being. Our Father has much, so very much, to say about that little member, the tongue. (James 3.) Give the devil no opportunity by getting into worry, unforgiveness, strife, and criticism. Put a stop to idle and foolish talking. (Ephesians 4:27; 5:4.) You are to be a blessing to others. (Galatians 6:10.)

Talk the answer, not the problem. THE ANSWER IS IN GOD'S WORD. You must have knowledge of that Word — revelation knowledge. (I Corinthians 2:7-16.)

As an intercessor, unite with others in prayer. United prayer is a mighty weapon that the Body of Christ is to use.

Believe you receive when you pray. Confess the Word. Hold fast to your confession of faith in God's Word. Allow your spirit by the Holy Spirit to pray. Praise God for the victory *now* before any manifestation. **Walk by faith and not by sight.** (II Corinthians 5:7.)

Don't be moved by adverse circumstances. As Satan attempts to challenge you, resist him steadfast in the faith — letting patience have her perfect work. (James 1:4.) Take the

7

Sword of the Spirit and the shield of faith and quench his every fiery dart. (Ephesians 6:16.) The entire substitutionary work of Christ was for you. Satan is now a defeated foe because Jesus conquered him. (Colossians 2:14-15.) He is overcome by the blood of the Lamb and the Word of our testimony. (Revelation 12:11.) Fight the good fight of faith. (I Timothy 6:12.) Withstand the adversary and be firm in faith against his onset — rooted, established, strong, and determined. (I Peter 5:9.) Speak God's Word boldly and courageously.

Your desire should be to please and to bless the Father. As you pray in line with His Word, He joyfully hears that you, His child, are living and walking in the Truth. (III John 4.)

How exciting to know that the prayers of the saints are forever in the throne room. (Revelation 5:8.) Hallelujah!

Praise God for His Word and the limitlessness of prayer in the name of Jesus. It belongs to every child of God. Therefore, run with patience the race that is set before you, looking unto Jesus the author and finisher of your faith. (Hebrews 12:1-2.) God's Word is able to build you up and give you your rightful inheritance among all God's set apart ones. (Acts 20:32.)

Commit yourself to pray and to pray correctly by approaching the throne with your mouth filled with His Word!

Introduction

"The earnest (heart-felt, continued) prayer of a righteous man makes tremendous power available — dynamic in its working" (James 5:16 *Amplified*).

Prayer is fellowshipping with the Father — a vital, personal contact with the God who is more than enough. We are to be in constant communion with Him *"for the eyes of the Lord are upon the righteous — those who are upright and in right standing with God — and His ears are attentive (open) to their prayer"* (I Peter 3:12 *Amplified*).

Prayer is not to be a religious form with no power. It is to be effective and accurate and bring *results*. God watches over His Word to perform it. (Jeremiah 1:12.)

Prayer that brings results must be based on God's Word. *"For the Word that God speaks is alive and full of power — making it active, operative, energizing and effective; it is sharper than any two-edged sword, penetrating to the dividing line of the breath of life (soul) and (the immortal) spirit, and of joints and marrow (that is, of the deepest parts of our nature) exposing and sifting and analyzing and judging the very thoughts and purposes of the heart"* (Hebrews 4:12 *Amplified*).

Prayer is this "living" Word in our mouth. Our mouth must speak forth faith for faith is what pleases God. (Hebrews 11:6.) We hold His Word up to Him in prayer, and our Father sees himself in His Word.

God's Word is our contact with Him. We put Him in remembrance of His Word (Isaiah 43:26) placing a demand on His ability in the name of our Lord Jesus. We remind Him that He supplies all of our needs according to His riches in glory by Christ Jesus. (Philippians 4:19.) That Word does not return to Him void — without producing any effect, useless — but it *shall* accomplish that which He pleases and purposes, and it shall prosper in the thing for which He sent it. (Isaiah 55:11.) Hallelujah!

God did *not* leave us without His thoughts and His ways for we have His Word — His bond. God instructs us to call Him and He will answer and show us great and mighty things. (Jeremiah 33:3.) Prayer is to be exciting — not drudging.

It takes someone to pray. God moves as we pray in faith — believing. He says that His eyes run to and fro throughout the whole earth to show himself strong in behalf of those whose heart is blameless toward Him. (II Chronicles 16:9.) We are blameless. (Ephesians 1:4.) We are His very own children. (Ephesians 1:5.) We are His righteousness in Christ Jesus. (II Corinthians 5:21.) He tells us to come boldly to the throne of grace and *obtain* mercy and find grace to help in time of need — appropriate and well-timed help. (Hebrews 4:16.) Praise the Lord!

The prayer armor is for every believer, every member of the Body of Christ, who will put it on and walk in it for the weapons of our warfare are *not carnal* but mighty through God for the pulling down of the strongholds of the enemy (Satan, the god of this world, and all his demonic forces). Spiritual warfare takes place in prayer. (II Corinthians 10:4, Ephesians 6:12.)

There are many different kinds of prayer, such as the prayer of thanksgiving and praise, the prayer of dedication and worship, and the prayer that changes *things* (not God). All prayer involves time of fellowshipping with the Father.

In Ephesians 6, we are instructed to take the Sword of the Spirit which is the Word of God and *"pray at all times — on every occasion, in every season — in the Spirit, with all manner (different kinds) of prayer and entreaty"* (Ephesians 6:18 Amplified).

In I Timothy 2 we are admonished and urged that *"petitions, prayers, intercessions and thanksgivings be offered on behalf of all men"* (I Timothy 2:1 *Amplified*). **Prayer is our responsibility.**

Prayer must be the foundation of every Christian endeavor. Any failure is a prayer failure. We are **not** to be ignorant concerning God's Word. God desires for His people to be successful, to be filled with a full, deep, and clear knowledge of His will (His Word), and to bear fruit in every good work. (Colossians 1:9-13.) We then bring honor and glory to Him. (John 15:8.) He desires that we know how to pray for *"the prayer of the upright is His delight"* (Proverbs 15:8).

Our Father has not left us helpless. Not only has He given us His Word, but also He has given us the Holy Spirit to help our infirmities when we know not how to pray as we ought. (Romans 8:26.) Praise God! Our Father has provided His people with every possible avenue to insure their complete and total victory in this life in the name of our Lord Jesus. (I John 5:3-5.)

We pray to the Father, in the name of Jesus, through the Holy Spirit, according to the Word!

Using God's Word on purpose, specifically, in prayer is one means of prayer, and it is a most effective and accurate means. Jesus said, *"The words (truths) that I have been speaking to you are spirit and life"* (John 6:63 *Amplified*).

When Jesus faced Satan in the wilderness, He said, *"It is written . . . it is written . . . it is written."* We are to live, be upheld, and sustained by every Word that proceeds from the mouth of God. (Matthew 4:4.)

James, by the Spirit, admonishes that we do not have because we do not ask. We ask and receive not because we ask amiss. (James 4:2-3.) We must heed that admonishment now for

11

we are to become experts in prayer rightly dividing the Word of Truth. (II Timothy 2:15.)

Using the Word in prayer is **not** taking it out of context, for His Word in us is the key to answered prayer — to prayer that brings results. He is able to do exceeding abundantly above all we ask or think, according to the power that works in us. (Ephesians 3:20.) The power lies within God's Word. It is anointed by the Holy Spirit. The Spirit of God does not lead us apart from the Word for the Word is of the Spirit of God. We apply that Word personally to ourselves and to others — not adding to or taking from it — in the name of Jesus. We apply the Word to the **now** — to those things, circumstances, and situations facing each of us **now.**

Paul was very specific and definite in his praying. The first chapter of Ephesians, Philippians, Colossians, and II Thessalonians are examples of how Paul prayed for believers. There are numerous others. *Search them out.* Paul wrote under the inspiration of the Holy Spirit. We can use these Spirit-given prayers today!

In II Corinthians 1:11, II Corinthians 9:14, and Philippians 1:4, we see examples of how believers prayed one for another — putting others first in their prayer life with *joy.* Our faith does work by love. (Galatians 5:6.) We grow spiritually as we reach out to help others — praying for and with them and holding out to them the Word of Life. (Philippians 2:16.)

Man is a spirit, he has a soul, and he lives in a body. (I Thessalonians 5:23.) In order to operate successfully, each of these three parts must be fed properly. The soul or intellect feeds on intellectual food to produce intellectual strength. The body feeds on physical food to produce physical strength. The spirit, the heart or inward man, is the real you, the part that has been reborn in Christ Jesus. It must feed on spirit food which is God's Word in order to produce and develop faith. As we feast upon God's Word, our minds become renewed with His Word, and we have a fresh mental and spiritual attitude. (Ephesians 4:23-24.)

Likewise, we are to present our bodies a living sacrifice, holy, acceptable unto God (Romans 12:1) and not let that body dominate us but bring it into subjection to the spirit man. (I Corinthians 9:27.) God's Word is healing and health to all our flesh. (Proverbs 4:22.) Therefore, God's Word affects each part of us — spirit, soul and body. We become vitally united to the Father, to Jesus and to the Holy Spirit — one with Them. (John 16:13-15, John 17:21, Colossians 2:10.)

God's Word, this spirit food, takes root in our hearts, is formed by the tongue, and is spoken out of our mouths. This is creative power. The spoken Word works as we confess it and then apply the action to it.

Be doers of the Word, and not hearers only, deceiving your own selves. (James 1:22.) Faith without works or corresponding action is *dead*. (James 2:17.) Don't be mental assenters — those who agree that the Bible is true but never act on it. **Real faith is acting on God's Word NOW.** We can't build faith without practicing the Word. We can't develop an effective prayer life that is anything but empty words unless God's Word actually has a part in our lives. We are to hold fast to our *confession* of the Word's truthfulness. Our Lord Jesus is the High Priest of our confession (Hebrews 3:1), and He is the Guarantee of a better agreement — a more excellent and advantageous covenant. (Hebrews 7:22.)

Prayer does not cause faith to work, but faith causes prayer to work. Therefore, any prayer problem is a problem of doubt — doubting the integrity of the Word and of the ability of God to stand behind His promises or the statements of fact in the Word.

We can spend fruitless hours in prayer if our hearts are not prepared beforehand. Preparation of the heart, the spirit, comes from meditation in the Father's Word, meditation on what we are in Christ, what He is to us, and what the Holy Spirit can mean to us as we become God-inside minded. As God told Joshua (Joshua 1:8), we meditate on the Word day and night, do according to all that is written, and then shall we make our way prosperous and have good success. We are to attend to God's Word, submit to His sayings, keep them in the center of our hearts, and put away contrary talk. (Proverbs 4:20-24.)

When we use God's Word in prayer, this is *not* something we just rush through uttering once, and we are finished. Do *not* be mistaken. There is nothing "magical" nor "manipulative" about it — no set pattern or device in order to satisfy what we want or think out of our flesh. Instead we are holding God's Word before Him. We confess what He says belongs to us.

We expect His divine intervention while we choose not to look at the things that are seen but at the things that are unseen for the things that are seen are subject to change. (II Corinthians 4:18.)

Prayer based upon the Word rises above the senses, contacts the Author of the Word and sets His spiritual laws into motion. It is not just saying prayers that gets the results, but it is spending time with the Father, learning His wisdom, drawing on His strength, being filled with His quietness, and basking in His love that bring results to our prayers. Praise the Lord!

Carolyn East

14

Prayers of Praise

"O magnify the Lord with me, and let us exalt His name together" (Psalm 34:3).

"As for God, His way is perfect! The Word of the Lord is tested and tried; He is a shield to all those who take refuge and put their trust in him" (Psalm 18:30).

"Let the words of my mouth and the meditation of my heart be acceptable in Your sight, O Lord, my firm impenetrable, rock and my redeemer" (Psalm 19:14).

"Your Word has revived me and given me life" (Psalm 119:50).

"Forever, O Lord, Your Word is settled in Heaven" (Psalm 119:89).

"Your Word is a lamp to my feet and a light to my path" (Psalm 119:105).

"The sum of Your Word is truth and every one of Your righteous decrees endures forever" (Psalm 119:160).

"I will worship toward Your Holy Temple, and praise Your name for Your loving-kindness and for Your truth and faithfulness; for You have exalted above all else Your name and Your Word, and You have magnified Your Word above all Your name!" (Psalm 138:2).

"Let my prayer be set forth as incense before You, the lifting up of my hands as the evening sacrifice. Set a guard, O Lord, before my mouth; keep watch at the door of my lips" (Psalm 141:2-3).

"He who brings an offering of praise and thanksgiving honors and glorifies Me; and he who orders his way aright —

15

who prepares the way that I may show him — to him I will demonstrate the salvation of God" (Psalm 50:23).

"My mouth shall be filled with Your praise and with Your honor all the day" (Psalm 71:8).

"Because Your loving-kindness is better than life, my lips shall praise You. So will I bless You while I live; I will lift up my hands in Your name" (Psalm 63:3-4).

"Your testimonies also are my delight and my counselors" (Psalm 119:24).

Prayers of Praise — taken from the Amplified Bible.

Personal Confessions

"Jesus is Lord over my spirit, my soul, and my body." (Philippians 2:9-11.)

"Jesus has been made unto me wisdom, righteousness, sanctification, and redemption. I can do all things through Christ who strengthens me." (I Corinthians 1:30, Philippians 4:13.)

"The Lord is my shepherd. I do not want. My God supplies all my need according to His riches in glory in Christ Jesus." (Psalm 23, Philippians 4:19.)

"I do not fret or have anxiety about anything. I do not have a care." (Philippians 4:6, I Peter 5:6-7.)

"I am the Body of Christ. I am redeemed from the curse for Jesus bore my sicknesses and carried my diseases in His own body. By His stripes I am healed. I forbid any sickness or disease to operate in my body. Every organ, every tissue of my body functions in the perfection in which God created it to function. I honor God and bring glory to Him in my body." (Galatians 3:13, Matthew 8:17, I Peter 2:24, I Corinthians 6:20.)

"I have the mind of Christ and hold the thoughts, feelings, and purposes of His heart." (I Corinthians 2:16.)

"I am a believer and not a doubter. I hold fast to my confession of faith. I decide to walk by faith and practice faith. My faith comes by hearing and hearing by the Word of God. Jesus is the author and the developer of my faith." (Hebrews 4:14, Hebrews 11:6, Romans 10:17, Hebrews 12:2.)

"The love of God has been shed abroad in my heart by the Holy Spirit and His love abides in me richly. I keep myself in the kingdom of light, in love, in the Word, and the wicked one touches me not." (Romans 5:5, I John 4:16, I John 5:18.)

"I tread upon serpents and scorpions and over all the power of the enemy. I take my shield of faith and quench his every fiery dart. Greater is He who is in me than he who is in the world." (Psalm 91:13, Ephesians 6:16, I John 4:4.)

"I am delivered from this present evil world. I am seated with Christ in heavenly places. I reside in the kingdom of God's dear Son. The law of the Spirit of life in Christ Jesus has made me free from the law of sin and death." (Galatians 1:4, Ephesians 2:6, Colossians 1:13, Romans 8:2.)

"I fear *not* for God has given me a spirit of power, of love, and of a sound mind. God is on my side." (II Timothy 1:7, Romans 8:31.)

"I hear the voice of the Good Shepherd. I hear my Father's voice, and the voice of a stranger I will not follow. I roll my works upon the Lord. I commit and trust them wholly to Him. He will cause my thoughts to become agreeable to His will, and so shall my plans be established and succeed." (John 10:27, Proverbs 16:3.)

"I am a world overcomer because I am born of God. I represent the Father and Jesus well. I am a useful member in the Body of Christ. I am His workmanship recreated in Christ Jesus. My Father God is all the while effectually at work in me both to will and do His good pleasure." (I John 5:4-5, Ephesians 2:10, Philippians 2:13.)

"I let the Word dwell in me richly. He who began a good work in me will continue until the day of Christ." (Colossians 3:16, Philippians 1:6.)

For our President and our Government

"Father, in Jesus' name, we give thanks for our country and its government. We hold up in prayer before You the men and women who are in positions of authority. We pray and intercede for the President, the representatives, the senators, the judges of our land, the policemen, as well as the governors and mayors, and for all those who are in authority over us in any way. We pray that the Spirit of the Lord rests upon them.

"We believe that skillful and godly wisdom has entered into the heart of our President and knowledge is pleasant to him. Discretion watches over him; understanding keeps him and delivers him from the way of evil and from evil men.

"Father, we ask that You compass the President about with men and women who make their hearts and ears attentive to godly counsel and do that which is right in Your sight. We believe You cause them to be men and women of integrity who are obedient concerning us that we may lead a quiet and peaceable life in all godliness and honesty. We pray that the upright shall dwell in our government . . . that men and women blameless and complete in Your sight, Father, shall remain in these positions of authority; but the wicked shall be cut off of our government and the treacherous shall be rooted out of it.

"Your Word declares that 'Blessed is the nation whose God is the Lord . . .' We receive Your blessing. Father, You are our refuge and stronghold in times of trouble (high cost, destitution and desperation). So we declare with our mouths that Your people dwell safely in this land and we *prosper* abundantly. We are more than conquerors through Christ Jesus!

"It is written in Your Word that the heart of the king is in the hand of the Lord and you turn it whichever way You desire.

We believe the heart of our leader is in Your hand and that his decisions are divinely directed of the Lord.

"We give thanks unto You that the good news of the gospel is published in our land. The Word of the Lord prevails and grows mightily in the hearts and lives of the people. We give thanks for this land and the leaders You have given to us, in Jesus' name.

"Jesus is Lord over the United States!"

SCRIPTURE REFERENCES:

I Timothy 2:1-3

Proverbs 2:10-12,21,22

Psalm 33:12

Psalm 9:9

Deuteronomy 28:10,11

Romans 8:37

Proverbs 21:1

Acts 12:24

For Nations and Continents

"Father, in the name of Jesus, we bring before You the nation (or continent) of _____ and its leaders. Father, You say in Your Word that you reprove leaders for our sakes so that we may live a quiet and peaceable life in all godliness and honesty.

"We pray that skillful and godly wisdom has entered into the heart of _____ leaders and that knowledge is pleasant to them; that discretion watches over them and understanding keeps them and delivers them from the way of evil and from the evil men.

"We pray that the upright shall dwell in this government . . . that men and women of integrity, blameless and complete in Your sight, Father, shall remain in it; but the wicked shall be cut off of this government and the treacherous shall be rooted out of it. We pray that those in authority winnow the wicked from among the good and bring the threshing wheel over them to separate the chaff from the grain for loving-kindness and mercy, truth and faithfulness preserve those in authority and their office is upheld by the people's loyalty.

"We confess and believe that the decisions made by the leaders are divinely directed by You, Father, and their mouths should not transgress in judgment. Therefore, the leaders are men and women of discernment, understanding, and knowledge so the stability of _____ will long continue. We pray that the uncompromisingly righteous be in authority in _____ so that the people there can rejoice. Father, it is an abomination to You and men for leaders to commit wickedness. We pray that their office be established and made secure by righteousness and that right and just lips are a delight to those in authority and that they love those who speak what is right.

"We pray and believe that the good news of the Gospel is published in this land. We thank You for laborers of the harvest to publish Your Word that Jesus is Lord in _____. We thank You for raising up intercessors to pray for _____ _____ in Jesus' name. Amen."

SCRIPTURE REFERENCES:

Psalm 105:14

Proverbs 2:10-15

Proverbs 2:21-22

Proverbs 20:26,28

Proverbs 21:1

Proverbs 16:10,12,13

Proverbs 28:2

Proverbs 29:2

I Timothy 2:1-2

Acts 12:24

Psalm 68:11

For School Systems
(Authority, Children, and Parent)

"Father, we thank You that the entrance of Your Word brings light and thank You that You watch over Your Word to perform it. Father, we bring before You the _____ school system(s) and the men and women _____ who are in positions of authority within the school system(s).

"We believe that skillful and godly wisdom has entered into their hearts; that Your knowledge is pleasant to them. Discretion watches over them; understanding keeps them and delivers them from the way of evil and from evil men. We pray that men and women of integrity, blameless and complete in Your sight, remain in these positions, but that the wicked be cut off and the treacherous be rooted out in the name of Jesus. Father, we thank You for **born-again, Spirit-filled people** in these positions.

"Father, we bring our children, our young people _____ _____ before You. We speak forth Your Word boldly and confidently, Father, that we and our households are saved in the name of Jesus. We are redeemed from the curse of the law for Jesus was made a curse for us. **Our sons and daughters are not given to another people.** We enjoy our children, and they shall not go into captivity in the name of Jesus.

"As parents, we train our children in the way they should go, and when they are old they shall not depart from it.

"Our children shrink from whatever might offend You, Father, and discredit the name of Christ. They show themselves to be blameless, guileless, innocent and uncontaminated children of God without blemish (faultless, unrebukable) in the midst of a crooked and wicked generation; holding out to it and offering to all the Word of Life. Thank You, Father, that You give them

23

knowledge and skill in all learning and wisdom and bring them into favor with those around them.

"Father, we pray and intercede that these young people _____, their parents _____, and the leaders in the school system(s) _____ separate themselves from contact with contaminating and corrupting influences. They cleanse themselves from everything that would contaminate and defile their spirit, mind, and body. We confess that they shun immorality and all sexual looseness — flee from impurity in thought, word or deed. They live and conduct themselves honorably and becomingly as in the open light of day. We confess and believe that they shun youthful lusts and flee from them in the name of Jesus.

"SATAN, WE SPEAK TO YOU IN THE NAME OF JESUS. WE BIND YOU, THE PRINCIPALITIES, THE POWERS, THE RULERS OF THE DARKNESS, AND WICKED SPIRITS IN HEAVENLY PLACES AND TEAR DOWN STRONGHOLDS USING THE MIGHTY WEAPONS GOD HAS PROVIDED FOR US IN THE NAME OF JESUS. WE BIND UP THAT BLINDING SPIRIT OF ANTICHRIST. WE BIND EVERY SPIRIT OF THE OCCULT — ASTROLOGY, WITCHCRAFT, EVERY FAMILIAR SPIRIT. WE BIND SEXUAL IMMORALITY, IDOLATRY, OBSCENITY, AND PROFANITY. WE BIND THOSE SPIRITS OF ALCOHOL, NICOTINE, AND DRUG ADDICTION. WE BIND WORLDLY WISDOM IN ANY FORM — EVERY OPPOSER TO THE TRUTH. WE BIND EVERY DESTRUCT-IVE, DECEITFUL, THIEVING SPIRIT. YOU ARE LOOSED FROM YOUR ASSIGNMENT AGAINST _____ IN THE NAME OF JESUS FOR THEY ESCAPE FROM THE SNARE OF THE DEVIL THAT HAS HELD THEM CAPTIVE.

"We commission the ministering spirits to go forth and police the area dispelling the forces of darkness.

"Father, we thank You that in Christ all the treasures of divine wisdom (of comprehensive insight into the ways and purposes of God), and all the riches of spiritual knowledge and enlightenment are stored up and lie hidden for us and we walk in Him.

"We praise You, Father, that we shall see _____ _____ walking in the ways of piety and virtue, revering Your name, Father. Those who err in spirit will come to understanding and those who murmur discontentedly will accept instruction in the Way, Jesus, to do the will of You and carry out Your purposes in their lives for You, Father, occupy first place in their hearts. We surround _____ with our faith.

"Thank You, Father, that You are the delivering God. Thank You, that the good news of the Gospel is published throughout our school system(s). Thank You for intercessors to stand on Your Word and for laborers of the harvest to preach Your Word in Jesus' name. Praise the Lord!"

SCRIPTURE REFERENCES:

Psalm 119:130	I Corinthians 6:18
Jeremiah 1:12	Romans 13:13
Proverbs 2:10-12	Ephesians 5:4
Proverbs 2:21,22	II Timothy 2:22
Acts 16:31	Matthew 18:18
Galatians 3:13	II Timothy 2:26
Deuteronomy 28:32,41	Hebrews 1:14
Proverbs 22:6	Colossians 2:3
Philippians 2:15,16	Isaiah 29:23,24
Daniel 1:17,9	I John 2:17
II Timothy 2:21	I John 5:21
II Corinthians 7:1	

For the Body of Christ

"Father, we pray and confess Your Word over the Body of Christ. We pray that they be filled with the full (deep and clear) knowledge of Your Will in all spiritual wisdom — that is, in comprehensive insight into the ways and purposes of God and in understanding and discernment of spiritual things; that they walk — live and conduct themselves in a manner worthy of You Lord, fully pleasing to You and desiring to please You in all things, bearing fruit in every good work and steadily growing and increasing in and by the knowledge of You — with fuller, deeper and clearer insight, acquaintance and recognition.

"We pray that the Body of Christ will be invigorated and strengthened with all power, according to the might of Your glory, to exercise every kind of endurance and patience (perseverance and forbearance) with joy, giving thanks to You, Father, who has qualified and made them fit to share the portion which is the inheritance of the saints (God's holy people) in the Light. You, Father, have delivered and drawn them to Yourself out of the control and the dominion of darkness and have transferred them into the kingdom of the Son of Your love, in whom they have their redemption through His blood, which means the remission of their sins.

"Father, You delight at the sight of the Body of Christ standing shoulder to shoulder in such orderly array and the firmness and the solid front and steadfastness of their faith in Christ — that leaning of the entire human personality on Him in absolute trust and confidence in His power, wisdom, and goodness. They walk — regulate their lives and conduct themselves — in union with and conformity to Him, having the roots of their being firmly and deeply planted in Him — fixed and founded in Him — being continually built up in Him, becoming increasingly more confirmed and established in the faith.

"Your people, Father, clothe themselves as Your own picked representatives, Your chosen ones, who are purified and holy and well-beloved by You by putting on behavior marked by tender-hearted pity and mercy, kind feeling, gentle ways and patience — which is tireless, long-suffering and have the power to endure whatever comes, with good temper. They are gentle and forbearing with each other and, if they have a difference (a grievance or complaint) against another, readily pardoning each other; even as You Lord have freely forgiven them, so do they also forgive.

"Your people put on love and enfold themselves with the bond of perfectness — which binds everything together completely in ideal harmony. They let the peace from Jesus act as umpire continually in their hearts — deciding and settling with all finality all the questions that arise in their minds — in that peaceful state to which they are called. They are thankful, appreciative, giving praise to You always.

"The Body of Christ lets the Word spoken by Christ the Messiah have its home in their hearts and minds and dwell in them in all richness, as they teach, admonish, and train each other in all insight, intelligence, and wisdom in spiritual songs, making melody to You, Father, with Your grace in their hearts.

"And whatever they do in word or deed, they do everything in the name of the Lord Jesus and in dependence upon His person, giving praise to You, Father, through Him!"

SCRIPTURE REFERENCES:
Colossians 1:9-14   Colossians 3:12-17
Colossians 2:5-7

27

For Israel

"Father, in the name of Jesus, we come before You in prayer and in faith believing that You watch over Your Word to perform it and that no Word of Yours returns to You void but it prospers in that for which You sent it. Therefore, Father, we come boldly and confidently into Your throne room and present the nation of Israel and the Jewish people before You.

"Father, You say that You will bless those who bless Israel, and we do bless this nation and its people in the name of Jesus. In accordance with Your Word, we say, *O Israel, hope in the Lord! For with the Lord, there is mercy and loving-kindness, and with Him is plenteous redemption. Break forth, joyously, sing together, for the Lord has comforted you. He has redeemed Jerusalem. Arise, shine, be radiant with the glory of the Lord, for your light is come, and the glory of the Lord is risen upon you! Your offspring shall be known among the nations and your descendants among the peoples. All who see you will recognize and acknowledge that you are the people whom the Lord has blessed. Behold your salvation comes in the person of the Lord Jesus.*

"Father, we praise You that the children of Israel shall return and seek You from the line of David, their King of Kings. They shall come in anxious fear to the Lord and to Your goodness in these latter days. Thank You, Father, that the children of Israel will confess Jesus is the Christ, the Messiah, the Son of God come in the flesh. We believe and confess that they will know Christ, the Messiah, is the Guarantee of a better, stronger, more excellent, and more advantageous covenant.

"The Body of Christ arouses the Jews — making them jealous so that they seek to appropriate the benefits of the good news of the Gospel, that Jesus is the Way. We thank You that the Jewish people will not persist in their unbelief and disobedience, but will be grafted in for You, God, have the power to graft them in again.

"Father, You are gracious and merciful, and the children of Israel, as written in Your Word, shall go out from spiritual exile of sin and evil into the homeland with joy led forth by the Lord and His Word with peace. Thank you, Father, in Jesus' name."

SCRIPTURE REFERENCES:

Jeremiah 1:12
Isaiah 55:11
Genesis 12:3
Psalm 130:7
Isaiah 52:9
Isaiah 60:1

Isaiah 61:9
Hosea 3:5
Hebrews 7:22
Romans 11:14,23
Isaiah 55:12
Matthew 18:18

For Ministers

"Father, in the name of Jesus, we pray and confess that the Spirit of the Lord shall rest upon _____ . . . the spirit of wisdom and understanding, the spirit of counsel and might, the spirit of knowledge. We pray that as Your Spirit rests upon _____ He will make him of quick understanding because You, Lord, have anointed and qualified him to preach the Gospel to the meek, the poor, the wealthy, the afflicted. You have sent _____ to bind up and heal the brokenhearted, to proclaim liberty to the physical and spiritual captives, and the opening of the prison and of the eyes to those who are bound. _____ shall be called the priest of the Lord. People will speak of him as a minister of God. He shall eat the wealth of the nations.

"We pray and believe that no weapon that is formed against _____ shall prosper and that any tongue that rises against him in judgment shall be shown to be in the wrong. We pray that You prosper_____ abundantly, Lord — physically, spiritually and financially.

We confess that _____ holds fast and follows the pattern of wholesome and sound teaching in all faith and love which is for us in Christ Jesus. _____ guards and keeps with the greatest love the precious and excellently adapted Truth which has been entrusted to him by the Holy Spirit who makes His home in _____.

"Lord, we pray and believe that, each and every day, freedom of utterance is given _____, that he will open his mouth boldly and courageously as he ought to do to get the Gospel to the people. Thank you, Lord, for the added strength which comes superhumanly that You have given him.

"We hereby confess that we shall stand behind_____

_____and undergird him in prayer. We will say only that good thing that will edify   _____. We will not allow ourselves to judge him, but will continue to intercede for him and speak and pray blessings upon him in the name of Jesus. Thank you, Jesus, for the answers. Hallelujah!"

SCRIPTURE REFERENCES:

Isaiah 11:2,3	II Timothy 1:13,14
Isaiah 61:1,6	Ephesians 6:19,20
Isaiah 54:17	I Peter 3:12

For Missionaries

"Father, we lift before You those in the Body of Christ who are out in the field carrying the good news of the Gospel — not only in this country but also around the world. We lift those in the Body of Christ who are suffering persecution — those who are in prison for their beliefs. Father, we know that You watch over Your Word to perform it, that Your Word prospers in the thing for which You sent it. Therefore, we speak Your Word and establish Your covenant on this earth. We pray here and others receive the answer there by the Holy Spirit.

"Thank You, Father, for revealing unto Your people the integrity of Your Word and that they must be firm in faith against the devil's onset, withstanding him. Father, You are their light, salvation, refuge, and stronghold. You hide them in Your shelter and set them high upon a rock. It is Your will that each prosper, be in good health, and live in victory. You set the prisoners free, feed the hungry, execute justice, rescue and deliver.

"WE BIND YOU SATAN, AND EVERY MENACING SPIRIT THAT WOULD STIR UP AGAINST GOD'S PEOPLE IN JESUS' NAME.

"We commission the ministering spirits to go forth and provide the necessary help for and assistance to these heirs of salvation. We and they are strong in the Lord and in the power of Your might quenching every dart of the devil in Jesus' name.

"Father, we use our faith covering these in the Body of Christ with Your Word. We say that no weapon formed against them shall prosper and any tongue that rises against them in judgment they shall show to be in the wrong. This peace, security and triumph over opposition is their inheritance as Your children. This is the righteousness which they obtain from You,

Father, which You impart to them as their justification. They are far from even the thought of destruction, for they shall not fear and terror shall not come near them.

"Father, You say You will establish them to the end — keep them steadfast, give them strength, and guarantee their vindication, that is, be their warrant against all accusation or indictment. They are not anxious beforehand how they shall reply in defense or what they are to say for the Holy Spirit teaches them in that very hour and moment what they ought to say to those in the outside world, their speech being seasoned with salt.

"We commit these our brothers and sisters in the Lord to You, Father, deposited into Your charge, entrusting them to Your protection and care for You are faithful. You strengthen them and set them on a firm foundation and guard them from the evil one. We join our voices in praise unto You Most High and silence the enemy and avenger. Praise the Lord! Greater is He who is in us than he who is in the world!"

SCRIPTURE REFERENCES:

Jeremiah 1:12

Isaiah 55:11

I Peter 5:9

Psalm 27:1,5

III John 2

I John 5:4-5

Psalm 146:7

Psalm 144:7

Matthew 18:18

Hebrews 1:14

Ephesians 6:10,16

Isaiah 54:14,17

I Corinthians 1:8

Luke 12:11-12

Colossians 4:6

Acts 20:32

II Thessalonians 3:3

Psalm 8:2

I John 4:4

For Meetings, Seminars, Bible Studies

"Father, in the name of Jesus, we openly confess that the Word of God will come forth boldly and accurately during the (*meeting*) and that the people who hear Your Word will not be able to resist the intelligence, the wisdom and the inspiration of the Holy Spirit that will be spoken through Your minister(s) of the Gospel.

"We confess that, as Your Word comes forth, an anointing of the Holy Spirit will cause people to open their spiritual eyes and ears and turn from darkness to light — from the power of Satan to You, God, and make Jesus their Lord.

"We commit this meeting to You, Father, we deposit it into Your charge — entrusting this meeting, the people that will hear, and the people that will speak into Your protection and care. We commend this meeting to the Word — the commands and counsels and promises of Your unmerited favor. Father, we know Your Word will build up the people and cause them to realize that they are joint heirs with Jesus.

"We believe, Father, that as Your Word comes forth, an anointing will be upon the speaker and (*name*) will be controlled completely by the Holy Spirit for the Word of God that is spoken is alive and full of power, making it active, operative, energizing, and effective, being sharper than any two-edged sword. We believe that every need of every person will be met spiritually, physically, mentally, and financially.

"We thank You, Father, and praise You that, because we have asked and agreed together, these petitions have come to pass. Let these words with which we have made supplication before the Lord, be near to the Lord our God day and night, that He may maintain the cause and right of His people in the (*meeting*) as each day of it requires! We believe all the earth's people will know that the Lord is God and there is no other! Hallelujah!''

SCRIPTURE REFERENCES:

James 5:16
Matthew 18:19
Ephesians 6:19
Acts 6:10
Ephesians 1:18

Acts 26:18
Acts 20:32
Hebrews 4:12
Philippians 4:19
I Kings 8:59-60

Prosperity For Ministering Servants

"Father, how we praise You and thank You for Your Word knowing that You watch over Your Word to perform it and no Word of Yours returns void, but accomplishes that which You please and it prospers in the thing for which You sent it.

"Father, in the name of Jesus, we pray, confess and believe according to Your Word that those in Your Body that have sown the seed of spiritual good among the people reap from the people's material benefits for Lord You directed that those who publish the good news of the Gospel should live and get their maintenance by the Gospel. We confess that Your ministers seek and are eager for the fruit which increases to the people's credit — the harvest of blessing that is accumulating to their account. The people's gifts are the fragrant odor of an offering and sacrifice which You Father welcome and in which You delight. You will liberally supply, fill to the full, the people's every need according to Your riches in glory in Christ Jesus.

"We confess that those then who receive instruction in the Word of God share all good things with their teachers, contributing to their support. We confess that Your people will not lose heart and grow weary and faint in acting nobly and doing right for in due time and at the appointed season they shall reap, if they do not loosen and relax their courage and faint. So then, as occasion and opportunity are open to the people, they do good to all people not only being useful and profitable to them, but also doing what is for their spiritual good and advantage.

"We confess that Your people are a blessing, especially to those of the household of faith — those who belong to God's family, the believers. Thus, we believe and confess Your people sow generously that blessings may come to someone. Your people then reap generously and with blessings for You God love, take pleasure in, prize above other things, and are unwilling to abandon or do without a cheerful, joyous, prompt-to-do-it giver — whose heart is in his giving. God, You are then able to make all grace, every favor and earthly blessing, come to Your people in abundance, so that they are always and under all circumstances and whatever the need, self-sufficient, possessing enough to require no aid or support and furnished in abundance for every good work and charitable donation.

"As Your people give, their deeds of justice and goodness and kindness and benevolence go on and endure forever. And God, You who provide the seed for the sower and bread for the eating, will also provide and multiply the people's resources for sowing and increase the fruits of their righteousness. Thus Your people are enriched in all things and in every way so that they can be generous and their generosity as it is administered by Your teachers will bring thanksgiving to God.

"As it is written, *'Give and it will be given to you, good measure, pressed down, shaken together and running over will men pour into your bosom. For with the measure you deal out it will be measured back to you.'* Praise the Lord!"

SCRIPTURE REFERENCES:

Jeremiah 1:12
Isaiah 55:11
I Corinthians 9:11,14
Philippians 4:17-19

Galatians 6:6-10
II Corinthians 9:6-11
Luke 6:38

To Be God-inside Minded

"I am a spirit, I have a soul, and I live in a physical body. My spirit is the candle of the Lord. God, my Father, is guiding me into all the truth through my spirit.

"I am a child of God, born of the Spirit of God, filled with the Spirit of God, and led by the Spirit of God. I listen to my heart as I look to my spirit inside me.

"The Holy Spirit gives direction to my spirit and illumination to my mind. He leads me in the way I should go in all the affairs of life. He leads me by an inward witness. The eyes of my understanding are being enlightened. Wisdom is in my inward parts. His love is perfected in me. I have an unction from the Holy One.

"I am becoming spirit-conscious. I listen to the voice of my spirit and obey what my spirit tells me. I let my spirit dominate me, for I walk not after the flesh, but after the spirit. I examine my leading in the light of His Word. I trust in the Lord with all my heart and lean not to my own understanding. In all my ways I acknowledge Him, and He directs my paths. I walk in the light of God's Word.

"I will educate and train and develop my human spirit. The Word of God shall not depart out of my mouth. I meditate therein day and night. Therefore I shall make my way prosperous, and I will have good success in life. **I am a doer of the Word and put God's Word first.** My spirit man is in the ascendancy.

"Thanks be unto God who always causes me to triumph in Christ!"

SCRIPTURE REFERENCES:

I Thessalonians 5:23	Job 38:36
Proverbs 20:27	I John 4:12
John 16:13	I John 2:20
Romans 8:14,16	Romans 9:1
John 3:6-7	Romans 8:1
John 7:37-39	Proverbs 3:5-6
Ephesians 5:18	Psalm 119:105
Isaiah 48:17	Joshua 1:8
Ephesians 1:18	James 1:22
I Corinthians 1:30	II Corinthians 2:14

To God's Word and an
Accurate Prayer Life

"Father, in the name of Jesus, **I commit myself to walk in the Word.** Your Word living in me produces Your life in this world. I recognize that Your Word is integrity itself — steadfast, sure, eternal — and I trust my life to its provisions.

"You have sent Your Word forth into my heart. I let it dwell in me richly in all wisdom. I meditate in it day and night so that I may diligently act on it. The Incorruptible Seed, the Living Word, the Word of Truth, is abiding in my spirit. That Seed is growing mightily in me now, producing Your nature, Your life. It is my counsel, my shield, my buckler, my powerful weapon in battle. The Word is a lamp to my feet and a light to my path. It makes my way plain before me. I do not stumble, for my steps are ordered in the Word.

"The Holy Spirit leads and guides me into all the truth. He gives me understanding, discernment, and comprehension so that I am preserved from the snares of the evil one.

"Father, Your eyes are over the righteous. Thus, Your ears are open to my prayers. **I am a person of prayer** — prayer rooted in Your Word. *I do have time to pray.* I am earnest and unwearied and steadfast in my prayer life, being both alert and intent in my praying with thanksgiving. I am an intercessor — a prayer warrior strong in the power of Your might. I refuse to turn coward — faint, lose heart and give up for **my prayers avail much** in the name of Jesus.

"I delight myself in You and Your Word. Because of that, You put Your desires within my heart. I commit my way unto You and You bring it to pass. I am confident that You are at work in me now both to will and to do all Your good pleasure.

"I exalt Your Word, hold it in high esteem, and give it FIRST place. **I make my schedule around Your Word,** I make the Word final authority to settle all questions that confront me. I choose to agree with the Word of God and I choose to disagree with any thoughts, conditions, or circumstances contrary to Your Word. I boldly and confidently say that my heart is fixed and established on the solid foundation — the living Word of God!"

SCRIPTURE REFERENCES:

Hebrews 4:12

Colossians 3:16

Joshua 1:8

I Peter 1:23

Psalm 91:4

Psalm 119:105

Psalm 37:23

Colossians 1:9

John 16:13

I Peter 3:12

Colossians 4:2

Ephesians 6:10

Luke 18:1

James 5:16

Psalm 37:4,5

Philippians 2:13

II Corinthians 10:5

Psalm 112:7,8

To Rejoice in the Lord

"Father, this is the day the Lord has made. I rejoice and I am glad in it! I rejoice in You always. And again I say, I rejoice. I delight myself in You, Lord. Happy am I whose God is the Lord!

"Father, You say that You rejoice over me with joy. Hallelujah! I am redeemed. I come with singing, and everlasting joy is upon my head. I obtain joy and gladness, and sorrow and sighing flee away. That spirit of rejoicing, joy, and laughter is my heritage. Where the Spirit of the Lord is there is liberty — emancipation from bondage, freedom. I walk in that liberty.

"Father, my mouth shall praise You with joyful lips. I am ever filled and stimulated with the Holy Spirit. I speak out in psalms and hymns and make melody with all my heart to You, Lord. My happy heart is a good medicine and my cheerful mind works healing. The light in my eyes rejoices the heart of others. I have a good report. My countenance radiates the joy of the Lord.

"Father, I thank You that I bear much prayer fruit. I ask in Jesus' name, and I will receive so that my joy (gladness, delight) may be full, complete, and overflowing. That joy of the Lord is my *strength*. Therefore, I can count it all joy, all strength, when I encounter tests or trials of any sort because I am strong in You, Father.

"I have the *victory* in the name of Jesus. Satan is under my feet. I am not moved by adverse circumstances. I have been made the righteousness of God in Christ Jesus. I dwell in the kingdom of God and have peace and joy in the Holy Spirit! Praise the Lord!"

SCRIPTURE REFERENCES:

Psalm 118:24

Philippians 4:4

Philippians 3:1

Psalm 144:15

Zephaniah 3:17

Isaiah 51:11

II Corinthians 3:17

James 1:25

Psalm 63:5

Ephesians 5:18,19

Proverbs 17:22

Proverbs 15:30

Philippians 4:8

Proverbs 15:13

John 15:7,8

John 16:23

Nehemiah 8:10

James 1:2

Ephesians 6:10

I John 5:4

Ephesians 1:22

II Corinthians 5:7

II Corinthians 5:21

Romans 14:17

To Walk in God's Wisdom and His Perfect Will

"Father, I thank You that the communication of my faith becomes effectual by my acknowledging every good thing which is in me in Christ Jesus. I hear the voice of the Good Shepherd. I hear my Father's voice, and the voice of a stranger I will *not* follow.

"Father, I believe in my heart and say with my mouth that **this day the will of God is done in my life.** I walk in a manner worthy of You Lord, fully pleasing to You and desiring to please You in all things, bearing fruit in every good work. Jesus has been made unto me wisdom. I single-mindedly walk in that wisdom expecting to know what to do in every situation, on *top* of every circumstance!

"I roll my works upon You, Lord, and You make my thoughts agreeable to Your will, and so my plans are established and succeed. You direct my steps and make them sure. I understand and firmly grasp what the will of the Lord is for I am not vague, thoughtless, or foolish. I stand firm and mature in spiritual growth convinced and fully assured in everything willed by God.

"Father, You have destined and appointed me to come progressively to know Your will — that is to perceive, to recognize more strongly and clearly and to become better and more intimately acquainted with Your will. I thank You, Father, for the Holy Spirit who abides permanently in me and who guides me into all the truth — the whole, full truth — and speaks whatever He hears from the Father and announces and declares to me the things that are to come. I have the mind of Christ and hold the thoughts, feelings, and purposes of His heart.

"So, Father, I have entered into that blessed rest by adhering, trusting, and relying on You in the name of Jesus. Hallelujah!"

SCRIPTURE REFERENCES:

Philemon 6

John 10:27,5

Colossians 1:9,10

I Corinthians 1:30

James 1:5-8

Proverbs 16:3,9

Ephesians 5:17

Colossians 4:12

Acts 22:14

I John 2:20,27

I Corinthians 2:16

Hebrews 4:10

John 16:13

To Walk in Love

"Father, in Jesus' name, I thank You that the love of God has been shed abroad, poured forth into my heart by the Holy Spirit Who has been given to me. I keep and treasure Your Word. The love of and for You, Father, has been perfected and completed in me, and perfect love casts out all fear.

"Father, I am Your child, and **I commit to walk in the God kind of love.** I endure long, am patient, and kind. I am never envious and never boil over with jealousy. I am not boastful or vainglorious, and I do not display myself haughtily. I am not rude and unmannerly and I do not act unbecomingly. I do not insist on my own rights or my own way for I am not self-seeking, touchy, fretful or resentful. I take no account of an evil done to me and pay no attention to a suffered wrong. I do not rejoice at injustice and unrighteousness, but I rejoice when right and truth prevail. I bear up under anything and everything that comes. I am ever ready to believe the *best* of others. My hopes are fadeless under all circumstances. I endure everything without weakening for my love never fails.

"Father, I *bless* and *pray* for those who persecute me — who are cruel in their attitude toward me. I bless them and do not curse them. Therefore, my love abounds yet more and more in knowledge and in all judgment. I approve things that are excellent. I am sincere and *without offense* till the day of Christ. I am filled with the fruits of righteousness.

"Everywhere I go I commit to plant seeds of love. I thank You, Father, for preparing hearts ahead of time to receive this love. I know that these seeds will produce Your love in the hearts to whom they are given.

"Father, I thank You that as I flow in Your love and wisdom, people are being blessed by my life and ministry.

Father, You make me to find favor, compassion and loving-kindness with others (*name them*).

"I am rooted deep in love and founded securely on love knowing that You are on my side, and nothing is able to separate me from the love of You, Father, which is in Christ Jesus my Lord. Thank You, Father, in Jesus' precious name. Amen."

SCRIPTURE REFERENCES:

Romans 5:5

I John 2:5

I John 4:18

I Corinthians 13:4-8

Romans 12:14

Matthew 5:44

Philippians 1:9-11

John 13:34

I Corinthians 3:6

Daniel 1:9

Ephesians 3:17

Romans 8:31,39

To Watch What You Say

"Father, today, I make a commitment to You in the name of Jesus. I turn from idle words and foolishly talking things that are contrary to my true desire to myself and toward others. Your Word says that the tongue defiles; that the tongue sets on fire the course of nature; that the tongue is set on fire of hell.

"In the name of Jesus, I am determined to take control of my tongue. I am determined that hell will not set my tongue on fire. I renounce, reject, and repent of every word that has ever proceeded out of my mouth against You God and Your operation. I cancel its power by dedicating my mouth to speak excellent and princely things and the opening of my lips for right things. My mouth shall utter truth.

"I am the righteousness of God, I set the course of my life for abundance, for wisdom, for health, and for joy. Everything I speak is becoming to God. I refuse to compromise or err from pure and sound words. The words of my mouth and my deeds shall show forth Your righteousness and Your salvation all of my days. I guard my mouth and my heart with all diligence. I refuse to give Satan any place in me. I am determined no longer to be double minded by the words of my mouth.

"Father, Your Words are first place to me. They are spirit and life. I let the Word dwell in me richly in all wisdom. The ability of God is released within me by the words of my mouth and by the Word of God. I speak Your Words out of my mouth. They are alive in me. You are alive and working in me. So, I can boldly say that my words are faith words, words of power, words of love, and words of life. They produce good things in my life and in the lives of others. Because I choose Your Words for my lips, I choose Your will for my life, and I go forth in the power of those words to perform them in Jesus' name."

SCRIPTURE REFERENCES:

Ephesians 5:4

II Timothy 2:16

James 3:6

Proverbs 8:6,7

II Corinthians 5:21

Proverbs 4:23

Proverbs 21:23

Ephesians 4:27

James 1:6

John 6:63

Colossians 3:16

Philemon 6

To Live Free from Worry

"Father, I thank You that I have been delivered from the power of darkness and translated into the kingdom of Your dear Son. **I commit to live free from worry in the name of Jesus** for the law of the Spirit of life in Christ Jesus has made me *free* from the law of sin and death.

"I humble myself under Your mighty hand that in due time You may exalt me casting the whole of my cares (*name them*) — all my anxieties, all my worries, all my concerns, once and for all — on You; for You care for me affectionately and care about me watchfully. You sustain me; You will never allow the consistently righteous to be moved — made to slip, fall, or fail!

"Father, I delight myself in You, and You perfect that which concerns me.

"I cast down imaginations (reasonings), and every high thing that exalts itself against the knowledge of You, and bring into captivity every thought to the obedience of Christ. I lay aside every weight, and the sin of worry which does try so easily to beset me. I run with patience the race that is set before me, looking unto Jesus, the author and finisher of my faith.

"I thank You, Father, that You are able to keep that which I have committed unto you. I think on (fix my mind on) those things that are true, honest, just, pure, lovely, of good report, virtuous, and deserving of praise. I let not my heart be troubled. I abide in Your Words, and Your Words abide in me. Therefore, Father, I do *not* forget what manner of man I am. I look into the perfect law of liberty and continue therein, being *not* a forgetful hearer, but a *doer of the Word* and thus blessed in my doing!

"Thank You, Father. *I am carefree.* I walk in that peace which passes all understanding in Jesus' name!"

SCRIPTURE REFERENCES:

Colossians 1:13	Hebrews 12:1,2
Romans 8:2	II Timothy 1:12
I Peter 5:6,7	Philippians 4:8
Psalm 55:22	John 14:1
Psalm 37:4,5	John 15:7
Psalm 138:8	James 1:22-25
II Corinthians 10:5	Philippians 4:6

From Corrupt Companions

*"SATAN, IN JESUS' NAME, TAKE YOUR HANDS OFF
_____. I BIND YOU FROM HIS LIFE. YOU
DESIST IN YOUR MANEUVERS AGAINST HIM."*

"Father, I thank You for delivering_____
from corrupt and depraved people. I confess that _____
_____ has awakened and returned to sober sense and his right
mind and sins no more. _____separates him-
self from contact with contaminating influences and cleanses
himself from everything that would defile his spirit, mind and
body.

" _____lives and conducts himself honor-
ably and becomingly as in the open light of day; not in reveling
(carousing) and drunkenness, not in immorality and debauchery
(sensuality and licentiousness), not in quarreling and jealousy.
_____is done with every trace of wickedness
(depravity, malignity) and all deceit and insincerity (pretense,
hypocrisy, and grudges and slander and evil speaking of every
kind.

" _____is loyally subject (submissive) to the
governing (civil) authorities — not resisting nor setting himself
up against them. _____is obedient, prepared
and willing to do any upright and honorable work. _____
_____ walks as a companion with wise men and he shall be
wise.

" _____ sins have been forgiven. _____
_____ is pardoned through the name of Jesus and
because of confessing His name. _____is
victorious over the wicked one because he has come to know and
recognize and be aware of the Father. The Word dwells and
remains in_____, and _____

dwells in the Son and in the Father always. God's nature abides in_____— His principle of life, the divine sperm, remains permanently within _____ and he cannot practice sinning because_____is born of God. The law of the Spirit of life in Christ Jesus has made _____free from the law of sin and death. Thank You, Father, for watching over Your Word to perform it in Jesus' name!''

SCRIPTURE REFERENCES:

I Corinthians 15:33-34a
II Timothy 2:21
II Corinthians 7:1
Romans 13:13
I Peter 2:1
Romans 13:1,2
Titus 3:1
Proverbs 13:20

Proverbs 28:7
I Thessalonians 5:22
I John 2:12-16
I John 2:21,24
I John 3:9
Romans 8:2
Jeremiah 1:12

From Satan and His Demonic Forces (Alcoholism, Gambling, Narcotics, the Occult, etc.)

If the person for whom you are interceding has not confessed Jesus as Savior and Lord, pray specifically for his salvation if you have not already done so. Stand and thank the Father that is is done in the name of Jesus. (See page 66 in book.) Then pray the following:

"Father, in the name of Jesus, I come boldly to Your throne of grace and present _____before You. I stand in the gap and intercede in behalf of_____ knowing that the Holy Spirit within me takes hold together with me against the evils that would attempt to hold_____ in bondage. I unwrap _____from the bonds of wickedness with my prayers and take my shield of faith and quench every fiery dart of the adversary that would come against _____.

"Father, You say that whatever I bind on earth is bound in heaven and whatever I loose on earth is loosed in heaven. You say for me to cast out demons in the name of Jesus.

"SO I SPEAK TO YOU, SATAN, AND TO THE PRINCIPALITIES, THE POWERS, THE RULERS OF THE DARKNESS, AND SPIRITUAL WICKEDNESS IN HIGH PLACES AND THE DEMONIC SPIRITS OF (name of spirits) ASSIGNED TO _____. I TAKE AUTHORITY OVER YOU AND BIND YOU AWAY FROM_____ IN THE MIGHTY NAME OF JESUS. YOU LOOSE_____ _____ AND LET HIM GO FREE IN THE NAME OF JESUS. I DEMAND THAT YOU DESIST IN YOUR MANEUVERS NOW. SATAN, YOU ARE SPOILED AND A DEFEATED FOE.

"Ministering spirits of God, you go forth in the name of Jesus and provide the necessary help to and assistance for

_____.

"Father, I have laid hold of _____ salvation and his confession of the Lordship of Jesus Christ. I speak of things that are not as though they were for I choose to look at the unseen — the eternal things of God. I say that Satan shall not get an advantage of _____: for I am not ignorant of Satan's devices. I resist Satan and he has run in terror from _____in the name of Jesus. I give Satan no place in _____. I plead the blood of the Lamb over_____for Satan and his cohorts are overcome by that blood and Your Word. I thank You, Father, that I tread on serpents and scorpions and over all the power of the enemy in _____behalf. _____is delivered from this present evil world. He is delivered from the powers of darkness and translated into the kingdom of Your dear Son!

"Father, I ask You now to fill those vacant places within _____with Your redemption, Your Word, the Holy Spirit, Your love, Your wisdom, Your righteousness, and Your revelation knowledge in the name of Jesus.

"I thank You, Father, that_____is redeemed by the blood of Jesus out of the hand of Satan. He is justified and made righteous by the blood of Jesus and belongs to You — spirit, soul and body. I thank You that every enslaving yoke is broken for_____will not become the slave of anything or be brought under its power in the name of Jesus. _____ has escaped the snare of the devil that has held him captive and henceforth does Your will, Father, which is to glorify You in his spirit, soul and body.

"Thank You, Father, that Jesus was manifested that He might destroy the works of the devil. Satan's works are destroyed in _____life in the name of Jesus. Hallelujah! _____walks in the kingdom of God which is righteousness, peace and joy in the Holy Spirit! Praise the Lord!"

Once this prayer has been prayed, thank the Father that Satan and his cohorts are bound. Stand firm, fixed, immovable, and steadfast on your confessions of faith as you intercede on this person's behalf for "**greater is He that is in you than he who is in the world**" (I John 4:4).

SCRIPTURE REFERENCES:

Hebrews 4:16

Ezekiel 22:30

Romans 8:26

Isaiah 58:6

Ephesians 6:16

Matthew 18:18

Mark 16:17

Ephesians 6:12

Colossians 2:15

Matthew 12:29

Hebrews 1:14

Romans 4:17

II Corinthians 4:18

II Corinthians 2:11

James 4:7

Ephesians 4:27

Revelation 12:11

Luke 10:19

Galatians 1:4

Colossians 1:13

Matthew 12:43-45

I Corinthians 6:12

II Timothy 2:26

I John 3:8

Romans 14:17

Of Loved Ones from Cults

"Father, in the name of Jesus, we come before You in prayer and in faith believing that Your Word runs swiftly throughout the earth for the Word of God is not chained or imprisoned. We bring before You_____ *(those and families of those involved in cults)*. Father, stretch forth Your hand from above, rescue and deliver_____ out of great waters, from the land of hostile aliens whose mouth speaks deceit and whose right hand is a right hand raised in taking fraudulent oaths. Their mouths must be stopped for they are mentally distressing and subverting _____ and whole families by teaching what they ought not teach, for the purpose of getting base advantage and disreputable gain. But praise God, they will not get very far for their rash folly will become obvious to everybody!

"Execute justice, precious Father, for the oppressed. Set the prisoners free, open the eyes of the blind, lift up the bowed down, heal the brokenhearted, bind up their wounds curing their pains and sorrow. Lift up the humble and down-trodden and cast the wicked down to the ground in the mighty name of Jesus.

"Turn back the hearts of the disobedient, incredulous, and unpersuadable to the wisdom of the upright, the knowledge, and holy love of the will of God in order to make ready for You, Lord, a people perfectly prepared in spirit, adjusted, disposed, and placed in the right moral state.

"Father, You say in Your Word to refrain our voice from weeping and our eyes from tears for our prayers shall be rewarded and _____shall return from the enemy's land and come again to their own country. You will save our offspring from the land of their exile, from the east and the west — sons from afar and daughters from the ends of the earth. We shall see _____walking in the ways of piety and virtue revering Your name, Father. Those who err in spirit will come to understanding. Those who murmur discontentedly will accept instruction in the Way, Jesus. Father, You contend with those who contend with us and You give safety to _____ and ease _____."

"SATAN, WE SPEAK TO YOU IN THE NAME OF JESUS. WE BIND YOU, THE PRINCIPALITIES, THE POWERS, THE RULERS OF THE DARKNESS, AND THE WICKED SPIRITS IN HEAVENLY PLACES, AND WE TEAR DOWN STRONGHOLDS USING THE MIGHTY WEAPONS GOD HAS PROVIDED FOR US IN THE NAME OF JESUS. WE SPEAK TO GREED, SELFISHNESS, PRIDE, ARROGANCE, BOASTFULNESS, ABUSE, BLASPHEMY, DISOBEDIENCE, UNGRATEFULNESS, PROFANITY, REBELLION, PERVERSENESS, SLANDER, IMMORALITY, FEROCITY, HATRED, TREACHERY, CONCEIT, LUST, MATERIALISM, ERROR, DECEIT, SPIRIT OF ANTICHRIST, UNWORTHINESS, FILTHINESS, CRUELTY, HOSTILITY, DEPRAVITY, DISTORTION, UNGODLINESS, AND FALSITY AND LOOSE YOU FROM ALL DIABOLICAL ASSIGNMENTS AGAINST _____. WE CANCEL ALL NEGATIVE TALKING AND DOUBT AND UNBELIEF. SATAN WILL NOT USE THIS AGAINST _____."

"We commission the ministering spirits to go forth and dispel these forces of darkness and bring _____ home in the name of Jesus.

"Father, we believe and confess that _____ has had knowledge of and been acquainted with the Word which was able to instruct _____ and give _____ _____ the understanding for salvation which comes through

58

faith in Christ Jesus. Lord, we pray and believe that You certainly will deliver _____ and draw_____ _____ to yourself from every assault of evil and preserve and bring_____safe into Your heavenly kingdom. Glory to You, Father, who delivers those for whom we intercede in Jesus' name!''

Once this prayer has been prayed for an individual, confess it as done. Thank the Father that he or she is delivered, returning from the enemy's land. Thank God that Satan is bound. Thank God for their salvation.

SCRIPTURE REFERENCES:

Psalm 147:15
II Timothy 2:9
Psalm 144:7-8
Titus 1:11
II Timothy 3:9
Psalm 146:7-8
Psalm 147:3-6
Luke 1:17
Jeremiah 31:16-17
Jeremiah 46:27

Isaiah 43:5-6
Isaiah 29:23-24
Isaiah 49:25
Matthew 18:18
II Timothy 3:2-9
Hebrews 1:14
II Timothy 3:15
II Timothy 4:18
Job 22:30

From Habits

"Father, in the name of Jesus and according to Your Word, I hereby believe in my heart and say with my mouth that Jesus is the Lord of_____life. I also confess that from this day forward_____is set free and delivered from the habit(s) of _____in the name of Jesus.

"SATAN YOU AND ALL YOUR PRINCIPALITIES, POWERS, AND MASTER SPIRITS WHO RULE THE DARKNESS, AND SPIRITUAL WICKEDNESS IN HIGH PLACES ARE BOUND UP AND _____IS LOOSED FROM YOU IN THE NAME OF JESUS, AS IT IS WRITTEN IN MATTHEW 18:18-19. NO LONGER CAN YOU, SATAN, HARASS OR OPERATE ANY OF YOUR UNCLEAN SPIRITS OR HABITS OVER _____. _____ WILL NOT BECOME THE SLAVE OF ANYTHING THAT EXALTS ITSELF OVER THE WORD OF GOD OR BE BROUGHT UNDER ITS POWER."

"I hereby confess that_____is strengthened and reinforced with mighty power in his innerself by the Holy Spirit that lives and dwells in his innermost being. _____ is strong in the Lord. He is empowered through his union with the Lord. He draws strength from the Lord . . . that strength which His boundless might provides_____ _____.

" _____arms himself with the full armor of God, that armor of a heavily armed soldier which God has supplied for him . . . his helmet of salvation . . . loins girded with truth . . . breastplate of righteousness . . . his feet shod with the preparation of the gospel of peace . . . his shield of faith . . . and the Sword of the Spirit, which is the Word of God. With God's armor on, _____is able to stand up against all the strategies and deceits and fiery darts of Satan in the name of Jesus.

"As an act of _____ will and _____ _____faith, he receives complete and total freedom NOW. He is set free and delivered because he has called upon the name of the Lord according to that which is written in His Word.

" _____is able to discipline his body and subdue it. He is strong. He is free. He withstands temptation because Jesus is the Lord of his life. Jesus is his High Priest and with Jesus and the Father on his side_____has the strength for all things . . . because greater is He that is in _____ than he that is in the world.

"Thank You, Lord. I praise You that _____ is whole and redeemed from every evil work. With You and Your Word in _____, _____ controls his body and its flesh. It does not nor can it ever again control him in the name of Jesus. Hallelujah!"

SCRIPTURE REFERENCES:

Romans 10:9-10,13

Matthew 18:18-19

I Corinthians 6:12

II Corinthians 10:4-5

Ephesians 3:16

Ephesians 6:10-17

Hebrews 4:14-16

I John 4:4

Romans 8:4,9

Romans 12:21

Romans 13:14

From Depression

"Father, You are my refuge and my high tower and my stronghold in times of trouble. I lean on and confidently put my trust in You; for You have not forsaken me who seeks You on the authority of Your Word and the right of my necessity. I ᴄᴄaise You, the help of my countenance and my God.

"Lord, You lift up those who are bowed down. Therefore, I am strong and my heart takes courage. I establish myself on righteousness — right, in conformity with Your will and order. I am far even from the thought of oppression or destruction, for I fear not; and from terror, for it shall not come near me.

"Father, You have thoughts and plans for my welfare and peace and *my mind is stayed on You* for I stop allowing myself to be agitated and disturbed and intimidated and cowardly and unsettled.

"SATAN, I RESIST YOU AND EVERY OPPRESSIVE SPIRIT IN THE NAME OF JESUS. I RESIST FEAR, DISCOURAGEMENT, SELF-PITY, AND DEPRESSION. I SPEAK THE WORD OF TRUTH, IN THE POWER OF GOD, AND I GIVE YOU NO PLACE, SATAN; I GIVE NO OPPORTUNITY TO YOU. I AM DELIVERED FROM OPPRESSION BY THE BLOOD OF THE LAMB.

"Father, I thank You that I have been given a spirit of power and of love and of a calm and well-balanced mind and discipline and self-control. I have the mind of Christ and hold the thoughts, feelings, and purposes of His heart. I have a fresh mental and spiritual attitude for I am constantly renewed in the spirit of my mind with Your Word, Father.

"Therefore, I brace up and reinvigorate and cut through and make firm and plain and smooth, straight paths for my feet

— safe and upright and happy paths that go in the right direction. I arise from the depression and prostration in which circumstances have kept me. I rise to new life. I shine and am radiant with the glory of the Lord.

"Thank You, Father, in Jesus' name that I am set free from every evil work. I praise You that the joy of the Lord is my strength and stronghold! Hallelujah!"

SCRIPTURE REFERENCES:

Psalm 9:9-10
Psalm 42:5,11
Psalm 146:8
Psalm 31:22-24
Isaiah 35:3-4
Isaiah 54:14
Isaiah 50:10
Jeremiah 29:11-13
Isaiah 26:3
John 14:27
James 4:7

Ephesians 4:27
Luke 4:18-19
II Timothy 1:7
I Corinthians 2:16
Philippians 2:5
Ephesians 4:23-24
Hebrews 12:12-13
Isaiah 60:1
Galatians 1:4
Nehemiah 8:10

To Receive Jesus as Savior and Lord

"Father, it is written in Your Word that if I confess with my mouth Jesus as Lord and believe in my heart that You have raised Him from the dead, I shall be saved. Therefore, Father, I confess that Jesus is my Lord. I make Him Lord of my life right now. I believe in my heart that You raised Jesus from the dead. I renounce my past life with Satan.

"I thank You for forgiving me of all my sin. Jesus is my Lord, and I am a new creation. Old things have passed away. Now all things become new in Jesus' name. Amen."

SCRIPTURE REFERENCES:
(to be shared with those to whom you are witnessing)

John 3:16
John 6:37
John 10:10b
Romans 3:23
II Corinthians 5:19
John 16:8,9
Romans 5:8

John 14:6
Romans 10:9-10
Romans 10:13
Ephesians 2:1-10
II Corinthians 5:17
John 1:12
II Corinthians 5:21

For Salvation (General)

"Father, it is written in Your Word, *First of all, then I admonish and urge that petitions, prayers, intercessions and thanksgivings be offered on behalf of* **all men** . . . .

"Therefore, Father, we bring the lost of the world this day, every man, woman, and child from here to the farthest corner of the earth, before You. As we intercede, we use our faith believing that thousands this day have the opportunity to make Jesus their Lord.

"FOR EVERYONE THAT HAS THAT OPPORTUNITY, SATAN, WE BIND YOUR BLINDING SPIRIT OF ANTI-CHRIST AND LOOSE YOU FROM YOUR ASSIGNMENT AGAINST THOSE WHO HAVE THAT OPPORTUNITY TO MAKE JESUS LORD.

"We ask the Lord of the harvest to thrust the perfect laborer across these lives this day to share the good news of the Gospel in a special way so that they will listen and understand it. We believe that they will not be able to resist the wooing of the Holy Spirit for You, Father, bring them to repentance by Your goodness and love.

"We confess that they shall see who have never been told of Jesus. They shall understand who have never heard of Jesus. And they shall come out of the snare of the devil that has held them captive. They shall open their eyes and turn from darkness to light — from the power of Satan to You, God!"

SCRIPTURE REFERENCES:

I Timothy 2:1-2
Job 22:30
Matthew 18:18

Romans 2:4
Romans 15:21
II Timothy 2:26

65

For Salvation (Specific)

"Father, in the name of Jesus, we come before You in prayer and in faith, believing. It is written in Your Word that Jesus came to save the lost. You wish **all men** to be saved and to know Your Divine Truth. Therefore, Father, we bring _____ _____ before You this day.

"SATAN, WE BIND YOU IN THE NAME OF JESUS AND LOOSE YOU FROM THE ACTIVITIES IN _____ *LIFE!*

"Father, we ask the Lord of the harvest to thrust the perfect laborer into his path, a laborer to share Your Gospel in a special way so that he will listen and understand it. As Your laborer ministers to him, we believe that he will come to his senses . . . come out of the snare of the devil that's held him captive and make Jesus the Lord of his life.

"Your Word says that You will deliver those for whom we intercede, who are not innocent, through the cleanness *of our hands.* We're standing on Your Word and from this moment on, Father, we shall praise You and thank You for his salvation. We have committed this matter into Your hands and with our faith we see _____ saved, filled with Your Spirit, with a full and clear knowledge of Your Word. Amen — so be it!"

Each day after praying this prayer, thank the Lord for this person's salvation. Rejoice and praise God for the victory! Confess the above prayer as done! Thank Him for sending the laborer. Thank Him that Satan is bound. Hallelujah!

SCRIPTURE REFERENCES:
Luke 19:10
Matthew 18:18
Matthew 9:38

II Timothy 2:26
Job 22:30

To Receive the Infilling
of the Holy Spirit

"My heavenly Father, I am Your child for I believe in my heart that Jesus has been raised from the dead and I have confessed Him as my Lord.

"Jesus said, *How much more shall your heavenly Father give the Holy Spirit to those that ask Him.* I ask You now in the name of Jesus to fill me with the Holy Spirit. I step into the fullness and power that I desire in the name of Jesus. I confess that I am a Spirit-filled Christian. As I yield my vocal organs, I expect to speak in tongues for the Spirit gives me utterance in the name of Jesus. Praise the Lord!"

SCRIPTURE REFERENCES:
(To be given to those with whom you are sharing)

John 14:16,17	Acts 10:44-46
Luke 11:13	Acts 19:2,5,6
Acts 1:8a	I Corinthians 14:2-15
Acts 2:4	I Corinthians 14:18,27
Acts 2:32,33,39	Ephesians 6:18
Acts 8:12-17	Jude 1:20

A Confession of Forgiveness for the Believer

"Father, in the name of Jesus, I make a fresh commitment to You to live in peace and harmony, not only with the other brothers and sisters of the Body of Christ, but also with my friends, associates, neighbors and family.

"I let go of all bitterness, resentment, envying, strife and unkindness in any form. I give no place to the devil in Jesus' name. Now Father, I ask Your forgiveness. By faith, I receive it, having assurance that I am cleansed from all unrighteousness through Jesus Christ. I ask You to forgive and release all who have wronged and hurt me. I forgive and release them. Deal with them in your mercy and loving-kindness.

"From this moment on, I purpose to walk in love, to seek peace, to live in agreement, and to conduct myself toward others in a manner that is pleasing to You. I know that I have right standing with You and Your ears are attentive to my prayers.

"It is written in Your Word that the love of God has been shed abroad, poured forth into my heart by the Holy Ghost who is given to me. I believe that love flows forth into the lives of everyone I know that I may be filled with and abound in the fruits of righteousness which bring glory and honor unto You, Lord, in Jesus' name. So be it!"

SCRIPTURE REFERENCES:

Romans 12:16-18,10   Ephesians 4:32
Philippians 2:2   I Peter 3:8,11,12
Ephesians 4:31,27   Colossians 1:10
I John 1:9   Romans 5:5
Mark 11:25   Philippians 1:9,11

Renew Fellowship

"Father, You hasten Your Word to perform it. I believe and confess that _____is a disciple of Christ, taught of You, Lord, obedient to Your will. Great is his peace and undisturbed composure. _____has You in person for his teacher. He has listened and learned from You and has come to Jesus.

" _____continues to hold to things he has learned and of which he is convinced. From childhood he has had knowledge of and been acquainted with the Word which is able to instruct him and give him the understanding of the salvation which comes through faith in Christ Jesus. Father, You will heal _____, lead _____, and recompense _____and restore comfort to _____.

"Jesus gives _____eternal life. He shall never lose it or perish throughout the ages, to all eternity. _____ shall never by any means be destroyed. No one is able to snatch _____out of Jesus' hand. You, Father, have given _____ to Jesus. You are greater and mightier than all else; no one is able to snatch _____ out of Your hand.

"I pray and believe that _____ comes to his senses and escapes out of the snare of the devil that has held him captive; and that _____ would judge himself.

"*IN THE NAME OF JESUS, SATAN AND EVERY HINDERING SPIRIT, YOU ARE BOUND IN _____ _____ LIFE.*

" _____ has become a fellow with Christ, the Messiah, and shares in all He has for him as he holds his first newborn confidence and original assured expectation firm and unshaken to the end. _____ casts not away his confidence for it has great recompense of reward.

"Thank You for giving _____ wisdom and revelation — quickening him to Your Word. Thank You that _____ enjoys fellowship with You and Jesus and with fellow believers."

SCRIPTURE REFERENCES:

Jeremiah 1:12

John 6:45

Isaiah 54:13

II Timothy 3:14-15

Isaiah 57:18

John 10:28-29

I John 5:16

II Timothy 2:26

I Corinthians 11:31

Matthew 18:18

Hebrews 3:14

Hebrews 10:35

Ephesians 1:17

I John 1:3

For Boldness

"Father, in the name of Jesus, I am of good courage. I pray that You grant to me that with all *boldness* I speak forth Your Word. I pray that freedom of utterance be given me that I may open my mouth to proclaim *boldly* the mystery of the good news of the Gospel — that I may declare it *boldly* as I ought to do.

"Father, I believe I receive that *boldness* now in the name of Jesus. Therefore, I have *boldness* to enter into the holiest by the blood of Jesus. Because of my faith in Him, I dare to have the *boldness* (courage and confidence) of free access — an unreserved approach to You with freedom and without fear. I can draw fearlessly and confidently and *boldly* near to Your throne of grace and receive mercy and find grace to help in good time for every need. I am *bold* to pray. I come to the throne of God with my petitions, and for others who do not know how to ascend to the throne.

"I will be *bold* toward Satan, demons, evil spirits, sickness, disease, and poverty for Jesus is the Head of all rule and authority — of every angelic principality and power. Disarming them that were ranged against us, He (Jesus) made a *bold* display and public example of them triumphing over them. I am *bold* to say, 'Satan, you are a defeated foe, for my God and my Jesus reign!'

"I take comfort and am encouraged and confidently and *boldly* say, 'The Lord is my Helper, I will not be seized with alarm — I will not fear or dread or be terrified. What can man do to me?' I dare to proclaim the Word toward heaven, toward hell, and toward earth.

"I am *bold* as a lion for I have been made the righteousness of God in Christ Jesus. I am complete in Him! Praise the name of Jesus!"

SCRIPTURE REFERENCES:

Psalm 27:14
Acts 4:29
Ephesians 6:19-20
Mark 11:23-24
Hebrews 10:19
Ephesians 3:12

Hebrews 4:16
Colossians 2:10,15
Hebrews 13:6
Proverbs 28:1
II Corinthians 5:21

On Improving Communication
with a Loved One

"_____ is a disciple of Christ — taught of the Lord and obedient to His will. Great is the peace and undisturbed composure of _____. _____ is constantly renewed in the spirit of his mind — having a fresh mental and spiritual attitude: and is putting on the new nature — the regenerate self — created in God's image, God-like in true righteousness and holiness.

"_____ life lovingly expresses truth in all things . . . speaking truly, dealing truly, living truly. _____ is enfolded in love, growing up in every way and in all things into Him, who is the Head, even Christ, the Messiah, the Anointed One. _____ mouth shall utter truth. _____ speaks excellent and princely things — the opening of his lips are for right things. All the words of his mouth are righteous. There is nothing contrary to truth or crooked in them.

"_____inclines his heart to Your testimonies, Father, and not to covetousness (robbery, sensuality or unworthy riches). _____ does not love or cherish the world. The love of the Father is in him. _____ is set free from the lust of the flesh (craving for sensual gratification), the lust of the eyes (greedy longings of the mind) and the pride of life (assurance in his own resources or in the stability of earthly things). _____ perceives and knows the truth and that nothing false is of the truth.

"_____ prizes Your wisdom, Father, and exalts it, and it will exalt and promote _____ . _____ attends to God's Words; consents and submits to Your sayings. _____ keeps them in the center of his heart. For they are life to _____ and medicine to all his flesh. _____ keeps his heart with all diligence for out of it flow the springs of life.

"_____ will do nothing from factional motives through contentiousness, strife, selfishness or for unworthy ends — or prompted by conceit and empty arrogance. Instead, in the true spirit of humility _____ does regard others as better than _____ does himself.

_____ esteems and looks upon and is concerned for not merely his own interests, but also for the interests of others.

"_____ lets this same attitude and purpose and humble mind be in him which was in Christ Jesus. Thank you, Father, in Jesus' name."

SCRIPTURE REFERENCES:

Isaiah 54:13
Ephesians 4:23,24
Ephesians 4:15
Proverbs 8:6-8

Psalm 119:36
I John 2:15,16,21
Proverbs 4:8,20-23
Philippians 2:2-5

For Those Involved in Court Cases

"Father, in the name of Jesus, it is written in Your Word to call on You and You will answer me and show me great and mighty things. I put You in remembrance of Your Word and thank You that You watch over it to perform it.

"I say that no weapon formed against me shall prosper and any tongue that rises against me in judgment I shall show to be in the wrong. This peace, security and triumph over opposition is my inheritance as Your child. This is the righteousness which I obtain from You, Father, which You impart to me as my justification. I am far from even the thought of destruction, for I shall not fear and terror shall not come near me.

"Father, You say You will establish me to the end — keep me steadfast, give me strength, and guarantee my vindication; that is, be my warrant against all accusation or indictment. Father, You contend with those who contend with me and You perfect that which concerns me. I dwell in the secret place of the Most High and this secret place hides me from the strife of tongues for a false witness who breathes out lies is an abomination to You.

"I am a true witness and all my words are upright and in rightstanding with You, Father. By my long forbearing and calmness of spirit the judge is persuaded and my soft speech breaks down the most bonelike resistance. Therefore, I am not anxious beforehand how I shall reply in defense or what I am to say for the Holy Spirit teaches me *in that very hour* and moment what I ought to say to those in the outside world — my speech seasoned with salt.

"I thank You, Father, that Satan and every menacing spirit are bound from operating against me for I am strong in You Lord and in the power of Your might quenching every fiery dart.

Thank You, Father, that I increase in wisdom and in stature and years, and in *favor* with You God and man. Praise the Lord!"

SCRIPTURE REFERENCES:

Jeremiah 33:3

Jeremiah 1:12

Isaiah 43:26

Isaiah 54:17

Isaiah 54:14

I Corinthians 1:8

Isaiah 49:25

Psalm 138:8

Psalm 91:1

Psalm 31:20

Proverbs 6:19

Proverbs 14:25

Proverbs 8:8

Proverbs 25:15

Luke 12:11-12

Colossians 4:6

Matthew 18:18

Ephesians 6:10,16

Luke 2:52

For Employment

"Father, in Jesus' name, we believe and confess Your Word over _____ today knowing that You watch over Your Word to perform it. Your Word prospers in _____ where into it is sent! Father, You are _____ source of every consolation, comfort, and encouragement. _____ is courageous and grows in strength.

"_____ desire is to owe no man anything but to love him. Therefore, _____ is strong and lets not his hands be weak or slack, for his work shall be rewarded. His wages are not counted as a favor or a gift, but as something owed to him. _____ makes it his ambition and definitely endeavors to live quietly and peacefully, minds his own affairs, and works with his hands so that he bears himself becomingly. He is correct and honorable and commands the respect of the outside world, being self-supporting, dependent on nobody and having need of nothing for You, Father, supply to the full his every need.

"He works in quietness, earns his own food and other necessities. He is not weary of doing right and continues in welldoing without weakening. _____ learns to apply himself to good deeds — to honest labor and honorable employment — so that he is able to meet necessary demands whenever the occasion may require.

"Father, You know the record of _____ works and what he is doing. You have set before _____ a door wide open, which no one is able to shut.

"_____ does not fear and is not dismayed for You, Father, strengthen him. You, Father, help _____ _____ in Jesus' name for in Jesus _____ has perfect peace and confidence and is of good cheer for Jesus

overcame the world — deprived it of its power to harm
_____. _____ does not fret or have
anxiety about anything for Your peace, Father, mounts guard
over his heart and mind. _____ knows the secret
of facing every situation for he is self-sufficient in Christ's
sufficiency. _____ guards his mouth and his
tongue keeping himself from trouble.

"_____ prizes Your wisdom, Father, and
acknowledges You. You direct, make straight and plain his path
and You promote him. Therefore, Father, _____
increases in Your wisdom (in broad and full understanding), and
in stature and years, and in favor with You, Father, and with
man!"

SCRIPTURE REFERENCES:

Jeremiah 1:12
Isaiah 55:11
II Corinthians 1:3
I Corinthians 16:13
Romans 13:8
II Chronicles 15:7
Romans 4:4
I Thessalonians 4:11,12
II Thessalonians 3:12,13
Luke 2:52

Titus 3:14
Revelation 3:8
Isaiah 41:10
John 16:33
Philippians 4:6,7
Philippians 4:12,13
Proverbs 21:23
Proverbs 3:6
Proverbs 4:8

For Finding Favor with Others

"Father, in the name of Jesus, You make Your face to shine upon and enlighten _____ and are gracious (kind, merciful, and giving favor) to _____. _____ is the head and not the tail. _____ is above only and not beneath.

"_____ who seeks Your Kingdom and Your righteousness and diligently seeks good, procures favor. _____ _____ is a blessing to You, Lord, and is a blessing to (*name them: family, neighbors, business associates, etc.*). Grace (favor) is with _____ who loves the Lord Jesus in sincerity. _____ extends favor, honor and love to (*names*). _____ is flowing in Your love, Father. You are pouring out upon _____ the spirit of favor. You crown him with glory and honor for he is Your child — Your workmanship.

"_____ is a success today. _____ is someone very special with You, Lord. _____ is growing in the Lord — waxing strong in spirit. Father, You give _____ knowledge and skill in all learning and wisdom.

"You bring _____ to find favor, compassion and loving-kindness with (*names*). _____ obtains favor in the sight of all who look upon him this day in the name of Jesus. _____ is filled with Your fullness — rooted and grounded in love. You are doing exceeding aboundantly above all that _____ asks or thinks for Your mighty power is taking over in _____.

"Thank You, Father, that _____ is
well-favored by You and by man in Jesus' name!"

SCRIPTURE REFERENCES:

Numbers 6:25
Deuteronomy 28:13
Matthew 6:33
Proverbs 11:27
Ephesians 6:24
Luke 6:38
Zechariah 12:10

Psalm 8:5
Ephesians 2:10
Luke 2:40
Daniel 1:17,9
Esther 2:15,17
Ephesians 3:19,20

For Safety

"Father, in the name of Jesus, I thank You that You watch over Your Word to perform it. I thank You that I dwell in the secret place of the Most High and that I remain **stable** and **fixed** under the shadow of the Almighty whose power no foe can withstand.

"Father, You are my refuge and my fortress. **No evil shall befall me — no accident shall overtake me — nor any plague or calamity come near my home.** You give Your angels special charge over me, to accompany and defend and preserve me in all my ways of obedience and service. They are encamped around about me.

"Father, You are my confidence, firm and strong. You keep my foot from being caught in a trap or hidden danger. Father, You give me safety and ease me — **Jesus is my safety!**

"**Traveling** . . . As I go, I say, 'Let me pass over to the other side,' and I have what I say. I walk on my way securely and in confident trust for my heart and mind are firmly fixed and stayed on You, and I am kept in perfect peace.

"**Sleeping** . . . Father, I sing for joy upon my bed. I lay me down, and You sustain me. In peace I lie down and sleep, for You alone, Lord, make me dwell in safety. I lie down and I am not afraid. My sleep is sweet for You give *blessings* to me in sleep. Thank You, Father, in Jesus' name. Amen."

Continue to feast and meditate upon all of Psalm 91 for yourself and your loved ones!

SCRIPTURE REFERENCES:

Jeremiah 1:12

Psalm 91:1,2

Psalm 91:10
(Swedish Translation)

Psalm 91:11

Psalm 34:7

Proverbs 3:26

Isaiah 49:25

Mark 4:35

Mark 11:23

Proverbs 3:23

Psalm 112:7

Isaiah 26:3

Psalm 149:5

Psalm 3:5

Psalm 4:8

Proverbs 3:24

Psalm 127:2

For Singles

"_____ is united to the Lord and has become one spirit with Him. _____ shuns immorality and all sexual looseness. _____ flees from impurity in thought, word or deed.

"_____ will not sin against his body by committing sexual immorality. _____ body is the temple of the Holy Spirit who lives within him, whom _____ has received as a gift from God. _____ is not his own. _____ was bought for a price, purchased with a preciousness and paid for, made God's own. _____ will honor God and bring glory to Him in his body and in his spirit which are God's.

"_____ shuns youthful lusts and flees from them, and aims at and pursues righteousness — all that is virtuous and good, right living, conformity to the will of God in thought, word and deed. He aims at and pursues faith, love and peace — which is harmony and concord with others — in fellowship with all Christians, who call upon the Lord out of a pure heart.

"_____ shrinks from whatever might offend You, Father, and discredit the name of Christ. _____ shows himself to be a blameless, guileless, innocent and uncontaminated child of God without blemish (faultless) in the midst of a crooked and wicked generation, among whom _____ is seen as a bright light shining out clearly — in the dark world, holding out to it and offering to all the Word of Life. Thank You, Father, that Jesus is Lord."

SCRIPTURE REFERENCES:

I Corinthians 6:17-20   Philippians 2:12,15,16
II Timothy 2:22

For a Single Female who is Trusting God for a Mate

"Father, in the name of Jesus, I believe that You are providing Your very best for _____. And, the man that will be united with _____ in marriage has awakened to righteousness. Father, as You have rejoiced over Jerusalem, so shall the bridegroom rejoice over _____. Thank You, Father, that he will love _____ as Christ loves the Church. He will nourish, carefully protect and cherish _____.

"Father, I believe because he is Your best that doubts, wavering and insincerity are not a part of him; but he speaks forth the oracles of God, acknowledging Your full counsel with all wisdom and knowledge. He does not speak or act contrary to the Word. He walks totally in love, esteeming and preferring others higher than himself.

"Father, I believe that everything not of You shall be removed from _____ life. And, I thank You for the perfecting of Your Word in _____ life that she may be thoroughly furnished unto all good works. Father, I praise You for the performance of Your Word in _____ behalf."

SCRIPTURE REFERENCES:

Isaiah 62:5   James 3:17
Ephesians 5:25   Proverbs 8:8

For a Single Male who is
Trusting God for a Mate

"Father, in the name of Jesus, I believe that You are providing a suitable helpmate for _____. Father, according to Your Word, one who will adapt herself to _____ _____, respect, honor, prefer and esteem him, stand firmly by his side, united in spirit and purpose, having the same love and being in full accord and of one harmonious mind and intention.

"Father, You say in Your Word that a wise, understanding and prudent wife is from You and he who finds a true wife finds a good thing and obtains favor of You.

"Father, I know that _____ has found favor in Your sight and I praise You and thank You for Your Word knowing that You watch over it to perform it."

SCRIPTURE REFERENCES:

Ephesians 5:22,33
Proverbs 18:22

Proverbs 19:14
Philippians 2:2

For the Spirit-controlled Life

"The law of the Spirit of life in Christ Jesus has made _____ free from the law of sin and death. _____ life is governed not by the standards and according to the dictates of the flesh but controlled by the Holy Spirit. _____ is not living the life of the flesh. _____ is living the life of the Spirit. The Holy Spirit of God dwells within _____ and directs and controls him.

"_____ is a conqueror and gains a surpassing victory through Jesus who loved him. _____ does not let himself be overcome by evil, but overcomes and masters evil with good. _____ has on the full armor of light. _____ clothes himself with the Lord Jesus Christ, the Messiah, and makes no provision for indulging the flesh.

"_____ is a doer of God's Word. He has God's wisdom. He is peace-loving, courteous, considerate, gentle, willing to yield to reason, full of compassion and good fruits. _____ is free from doubts, wavering and insincerity. He is subject to God.

"_____ stands firm against the devil. _____ resists the devil and he flees from _____. _____ comes close to God and God comes close to him. _____ does not fear for God never leaves him.

"In Christ, _____ is filled with the Godhead: Father, Son, and Holy Spirit. Jesus is _____ **Lord!**"

SCRIPTURE REFERENCES:

Romans 8:2,4,9,14,31,37　　James 3:17
Romans 12:21　　Hebrews 13:5
Romans 13:12,14　　James 4:7,8
James 1:22　　Colossians 2:10

For Victory over Fear

"Father, in Jesus' name, I confess and believe that no weapon formed against me shall prosper and any tongue that rises against me in judgment I shall show to be in the wrong. I believe I dwell in the secret place of the Most High. I shall remain stable and fixed under the shadow of the Almighty God whose power no foe can withstand — this secret place hides me from the strife of tongues.

"I believe the wisdom of God's Word dwells in me and, because it does, I realize that I am without fear or dread of evil. In all my ways I know and acknowledge God and His Word; thus, He directs and makes straight and plain my pathway. As I attend to God's Word, it is health to my nerves and sinews and marrow and moistening to my bones.

"I am strengthened and reinforced with mighty power in my innerself by the Holy Spirit himself that dwells in me. God is my strength and my refuge and I confidently trust in Him and in His Word. I am empowered through my union with Almighty God. (This gives me the superhuman, supernatural strength to walk in divine health and to live in abundance.)

"God himself has said, *I will never leave you without support or forsake you or let you down, my child. I will not, I will not, I will not in any degree leave you helpless or relax my hold on you . . . assuredly not!*

"I take comfort and am encouraged and confidently and boldly say, 'The Lord is my helper, I will not be seized with alarm, I will not fear or be terrified, for what can man do to me?'

"I confess and believe that my children are disciples taught of the Lord and obedient to God's will. Great is the peace and

87

undisturbed composure of my children — because God himself contends with that which contends with me and my children and He gives them safety and eases them. God will perfect that which concerns me.

"This Word of God that I have spoken is alive and full of power. It is active and operative. It energizes me and it affects me. As I speak God's Word, it is sharper than any two-edged sword and it is penetrating into my joints and into the marrow of my bones. It is healing to my flesh. It is prosperity for me. It is the magnificent Word of Almighty God. According to His Word that I have spoken, so be it! Hallelujah!"

SCRIPTURE REFERENCES:

Isaiah 54:17

Psalm 91:1

Psalm 31:20

Proverbs 3:6,8

Ephesians 3:16

Psalm 91:2

Ephesians 6:10

Hebrews 13:5,6

Isaiah 54:13

Isaiah 49:25

Psalm 138:8

Hebrews 4:12

For Victory over Gluttony

"Father, it is written in Your Word that if I confess with my lips that Jesus is Lord and believe in my heart that You have raised Him from the dead, I shall be saved. Father, I am Your child and confess that Jesus Christ is Lord over my spirit, my soul, and my body. I make Him Lord over every situation in my life. Therefore, I can do all things through Christ who strengthens me.

"Father, *I have made a quality decision to give You my appetite.* I choose *Jesus* rather than the indulgence of my flesh. I command my body to get in line with Your Word. I eat only as much as is sufficient for me. I eat and am satisfied. When I sit down to eat, I consider what is before me. I am *not* given to the desire of dainties or deceitful foods.

"Like a boxer, I buffet my body — handle it roughly, discipline it by hardships — and subdue it. I bring my body into subjection to my spirit man — the inward man — the real me. Not all things are helpful — good for me to do though permissible. I will not become the slave of anything or be brought under its power.

"My body is for the Lord. I dedicate my body — presenting all my members and faculties — as a living sacrifice, holy and well pleasing to You. I offer or yield myself and my bodily members and faculties to You, presenting them as implements of righteousness. I am united to You, Lord, and become one spirit with You. My body is the temple, the very sanctuary, of the Holy Spirit who lives within me, whom I have received as a gift from You, Father.

"I am not my own. I was bought for a price, made Your own. So then, I honor You and bring glory to You in my body. Therefore, I always exercise and discipline myself — mortifying my body (deadening my carnal affections, bodily appetites, and worldly desires) endeavoring in all respects — to have a clean (unshaken, blameless) conscience, void of offense toward You, Father, and toward men. I keep myself from idols — false gods, (from anything and everything that would occupy the place in my heart due to You, from any sort of substitute for You that would take first place in my life).

"I no longer spend the rest of my natural life living by my human appetites and desires, but I live for what You will! I am on my guard. I refuse to be overburdened and depressed, weighed down with the giddiness and headache and nausea of self-indulgence, drunkenness (on food), worldly worries and cares, for I have been given a spirit of power and of love and of calm and well-balanced mind and discipline and self-control.

"Father, I *do* resist temptation in the name of Jesus. I strip off and throw aside every encumbrance — unnecessary weight — and this gluttony which so readily (deftly and cleverly) tries to cling to and entangle me. I run with patient endurance and steady and active persistance the appointed course of the race that is set before me, looking away (from all that will distract) to Jesus the author and finisher of my faith.

"Christ the Messiah **will** be magnified and get glory and praise in this body of mine and **will** be boldly exalted in my person. Thank you, Father, in Jesus' name! Hallelujah!"

SCRIPTURE REFERENCES:

Romans 10:9,10	Proverbs 23:1-3	Luke 21:34
Philippians 4:13	Romans 6:13	II Timothy 1:7
Deuteronomy 30:19	I Corinthians 9:27	James 4:7
Romans 13:14	I Corinthians 6:19,20	Hebrews 12:1,2
Proverbs 25:16	Romans 12:1	Philippians 1:20
I Corinthians 6:12,13,17		

For Health and Healing

"Father, in the name of Jesus, we confess Your Word concerning healing. As we do this, we believe and say that Your Word will not return to You void, but will accomplish what it says it will. Therefore, we believe in the name of Jesus that _____ is healed according to I Peter 2:24. It is written in Your Word that Jesus himself took his infirmities and bore his sicknesses. (Matthew 8:17.) Therefore, with great boldness and confidence we say on the authority of that written Word that _____ is redeemed from the curse of sickness and _____ refuses to tolerate its symptoms.

"SATAN, WE SPEAK TO YOU IN THE NAME OF JESUS AND SAY THAT YOUR PRINCIPALITIES, POWERS, YOUR MASTER SPIRITS WHO RULE THE PRESENT DARKNESS, AND YOUR SPIRITUAL WICKEDNESS IN HEAVENLY PLACES ARE BOUND FROM OPERATING AGAINST _____ IN ANY WAY. _____ IS LOOSED FROM YOUR ASSIGNMENT. _____ IS THE PROPERTY OF ALMIGHTY GOD AND WE GIVE YOU NO PLACE IN _____. _____ DWELLS IN THE SECRET PLACE OF THE MOST HIGH GOD; _____ ABIDES, REMAINS STABLE AND FIXED UNDER THE SHADOW OF THE ALMIGHTY, WHOSE POWER NO FOE CAN WITHSTAND.

"Now, Father, because we reverence and worship You, we have the assurance of Your Word that the angel of the Lord encamps around about _____ and delivers _____ from every evil work. No evil shall befall _____, no plague or calamity shall come near his dwelling. We confess the Word of God abides in

_____ and delivers to him perfect soundness of mind and wholeness in body and spirit from the deepest parts of his nature in his immortal spirit even to the joints and marrow of his bones. That Word is medication and life to his flesh for the law of the Spirit of life operates in _____ and makes him free from the law of sin and death.

"We and _____ have on the whole armor of God and the shield of faith protects us from all the fiery darts of the wicked. Jesus is the High Priest of our confession, and we hold fast to our confession of faith in Your Word. We stand immovable and fixed in full assurance that _____ has health and healing NOW in the name of Jesus."

Once this has been prayed, thank the Father that Satan is bound and continue to confess this healing and thank God for it.

SCRIPTURE REFERENCES:

Isaiah 55:11
Galatians 3:13
James 4:7
Ephesians 6:12
II Corinthians 10:4
Psalm 91:1,10
Psalm 34:7

II Timothy 1:7
Hebrews 4:12,14
Proverbs 4:22
Romans 8:2
Ephesians 6:11,16
Psalm 112:7

Prayer for Those called Handicapped

"Father, we come before you boldly and confidently knowing that You are not a man that You should lie and that You watch over Your Word to perform it. Therefore, Father, we bring before You those who are called handicapped and ill — mentally and physically. Father, by the authority of Your Word, we know without a doubt that it is Your will for these people — babies, children, and adults — to be made completely whole and restored in the name of Jesus.

"We know, Father, that Satan, the god of this world, comes against Your handiwork. We know that You are the God of miracles, the God of love, and power, and might. Through Your redemptive plan, what Jesus did on the cross and in the pit of hell for us, we, Your people, are redeemed from the curse of the law. The law of the Spirit of life in Christ Jesus has made us free from the law of sin and death. We are seated with Christ in heavenly places far above all satanic forces.

"So we bring these people before Your throne of grace who have been attacked mercilessly — mentally and physically — by Satan and his cohorts. We intercede in behalf of them and their families and loved ones.

"*SATAN, WE SPEAK TO YOU AND TO THE PRINCIPALITIES, POWERS, RULERS OF THE DARKNESS OF THIS WORLD, AND WICKED SPIRITS IN HEAVENLY PLACES, AND WE BIND YOU AND LOOSE YOU FROM YOUR ASSIGNMENTS AGAINST THESE PEOPLE IN THE MIGHTY NAME OF THE LORD JESUS. YOU CAN NO LONGER HARASS OR HINDER THESE PEOPLE WHO HAVE THE OPPORTUNITY THIS DAY TO MAKE JESUS THEIR LORD AND SAVIOR. WE BIND DOUBT, UNBELIEF, FEAR, TRADITION, DISCOURAGEMENT,*

93

DEPRESSION AND OPPRESSION FROM OPERATING
AGAINST THE PARENTS, CHILDREN, AND
INDIVIDUALS INVOLVED.

"Father, we pray for born-again, Spirit-filled people in positions of authority — administrators, teachers, doctors, nurses, orderlies, attendants, and volunteers. We pray that men and women of integrity, blameless and complete in Your sight, remain in these positions, but that the wicked be cut off and the treacherous be rooted out. Father, we pray for laborers of the harvest to go forth preaching the good news to the lost and to the Body of Christ. We pray that You quicken these people to Your Word — that they be filled with wisdom and revelation knowledge concerning the integrity of Your Word, speaking faith-filled words and doing faith-filled actions, the infilling of the Holy Spirit, divine health, the fruit of the recreated human spirit, the gifts of the Holy Spirit, and deliverance. May they know that Jesus is their Source of every consolation, comfort, and encouragement and that they are to be sanctified spirit, soul, and body. We confess that they are redeemed from the curse of the law — redeemed from every sickness, disease, malady, affliction, defect, deficiency, deformity, injury and every demon.

"We speak healing to unborn infants in the wombs of mothers for 'Lo children are a heritage from the Lord, the fruit of the womb a reward, and blessed.'

"We speak restoration to damaged brain cells and activation of dormant brain cells. We speak normal intellect for one's age. We speak creative miracles to the parts of the body. We speak healing to all wounds. We speak words of life and say that you shall live in victory in this life and not die. We speak perfect soundness of mind and wholeness in body and spirit. We say that tongues are loosed and speech is distinct. We say ears hear and eyes see in the name of Jesus. We say demons are cast out bowing to the name of Jesus. We speak deliverance to bodies

94

and minds, for You, Lord God, are the help of their countenance and the lifter of those bowed down — the joy of the Lord is their strength and stronghold!

We commission God's ministering spirits to go forth as they hearken to God's Word to provide the necessary help for and assistance to those we are praying for!

"Father, no Word of Yours is void of the power that it takes to cause itself to come to pass! We establish Your Word on this earth for it is already forever settled in heaven. Nothing is too hard or impossible for You. All things are possible to us who believe. We pray for more intercessors to stand with us. Let our prayers be set forth as incense before You — a sweet fragrance to You! Praise the Lord!"

SCRIPTURE REFERENCES:

Romans 3:4	Mark 16:17	Mark 11:23-24
Jeremiah 1:12	Psalm 42:11	I Peter 2:24
Acts 3:16	Psalm 146:8	Matthew 8:17
II Corinthians 4:4	Nehemiah 8:10	Mark 7:35
John 10:10	Psalm 103:20	Proverbs 20:12
Galatians 3:13	Matthew 9:37-38	Luke 1:37
Romans 8:2	Ephesians 1:17-18	Psalm 119:89
Ephesians 2:6	II Corinthians 1:3	Jeremiah 32:27
Matthew 18:18	I Thessalonians 5:23	Mark 9:23
Proverbs 2:21-22	Psalm 127:3	Psalm 141:2

For Children and Parents

"Father, in the name of Jesus, I pray and confess Your Word over my children and surround them with my faith — faith in Your Word that You watch over it to perform it! I confess and believe that my children are disciples of Christ taught of the Lord and obedient to Your will. Great is the peace and undisturbed composure of my children . . . because You God contend with that which contends with my children and You give them safety and ease them.

"Father, You will perfect that which concerns me. *I commit and cast the care of my children once and for all over on You, Father.* They are in Your hands, and I am positively persuaded that You are able to guard and keep that which I have committed to You. **You are more than enough!**

"I confess that my children obey their parents in the Lord as His representatives for this is just and right. My children _____ honor, esteem, and value as precious their parents; for this is the first commandment with a promise: that all may be well with my children and that they may live long on earth. I believe and confess that my children choose life and love You, Lord, obey Your voice, and cling to You; for You are their life and the length of their days. Therefore, my children are the head and not the tail and shall be above only and not beneath and are blessed when they come in and when they go out.

"I believe and confess that You give Your angels charge over my children to accompany and defend and preserve them in all their ways. You, Lord, are their refuge and fortress. You are their glory and the lifter of their heads.

"As parents, we will not provoke, irritate, or fret our children. We will not be hard on them or harass them, or cause them to become discouraged, sullen, morose and feel inferior and frustrated. We will not break or wound their spirit, but we will rear them tenderly in the training, discipline, counsel and admonition of the Lord. We will train them in the way they should go and when they are old they will not depart from it.

"O Lord, my Lord, how excellent (majestic and glorious) is Your name in all the earth! You have set Your glory on or above the heavens. Out of the mouth of babes and unweaned infants You have established strength because of Your foes, that You might silence the enemy and the avenger. I sing praise to Your name, O Most High. **The enemy is turned back from my children in the name of Jesus!** _____ increases in wisdom and in favor with God and man."

SCRIPTURE REFERENCES:

Jeremiah 1:12

Isaiah 54:13

Isaiah 49:25

I Peter 5:7

II Timothy 1:12

Ephesians 6:1-3

Deuteronomy 30:19-20

Deuteronomy 28:13,3,6

Psalm 91:11,2

Psalm 3:3

Colossians 3:21

Ephesians 6:4

Proverbs 22:6

Psalm 8:1-2

Psalm 9:2-3

Luke 2:52

For the Home

"Father, I thank You that You have blessed me with all spiritual blessings in Christ Jesus.

"Through skillful and godly wisdom is my house (my life, my home, my family) built, and by understanding it is established on a sound and good foundation. And by knowledge shall the chambers (of its every area) be filled with all precious and pleasant riches — great priceless treasure. The house of the uncompromisingly righteous shall stand. Prosperity and welfare are in my house in the name of Jesus.

"My house is securely built. It is founded on a rock — revelation knowledge of Your Word, Father. Jesus is my Cornerstone. Jesus is Lord of my household. Jesus is Lord of us (_____) — spirit, soul, and body.

"Whatever may be our task we work at it heartily as something done for You, Lord, and not for men. We love each other with the God kind of love, and we dwell in peace. My home is deposited into Your charge, entrusted to Your protection and care.

"**Father, as for me and my house we shall serve the Lord in Jesus' name.** Hallelujah!"

SCRIPTURE REFERENCES:

Ephesians 1:3

Proverbs 24:3,4

Proverbs 15:6

Proverbs 12:7

Psalm 112:3

Luke 6:48

Acts 4:11

Acts 16:31

Philippians 2:10,11

Colossians 3:23

Colossians 3:14,15

Acts 20:32

Joshua 24:15

For Husbands

"Father, in the name of Jesus, I take Your Word and confess this day that _____ hearkens to the wisdom of God and that he and I shall dwell securely and in confident trust and shall be quiet without fear or dread of evil. _____ makes his ear attentive to skillful and godly wisdom and inclines and directs his heart and mind to understanding. He applies all of his power to the quest of it.

"He lets not mercy, kindness, and truth forsake him. He binds them about his neck and writes them on the tablet of his heart. He prizes the wisdom of God highly and exalts her. She will exalt and promote him — she will bring him to honor because he has embraced her. For the Lord is his confidence firm and strong and shall keep his foot from being caught in a trap or hidden danger.

"When _____ goes, the Word or wisdom of God shall lead him. When he sleeps, it shall keep him. When he wakes, it shall talk to him. Therefore, he will speak excellent and princely things and the opening of his lips shall be for right things. All the words of his mouth are righteous — upright and in right standing with God — and there is nothing contrary to truth or crooked in them.

"_____ will live considerately with me — with an intelligent recognition of our marriage relationship. He will honor me as physically the weaker. However, he does realize that we are joint heirs to the throne with Jesus spiritually. He does this in order that our prayers will not be hindered or cut off.

"I confess that we are of one and the same mind, united in spirit, compassionate and courteous, tenderhearted and humble-minded. I believe for our welfare, happiness, and protection because _____ and I love and respect each other.

"Thank you, Father, that _____ is a man of good report — that he is successful in everything he sets his hand to. He is uncompromisingly righteous. He captures human lives for God as a fisher of men. As he does this, he has the confidence that You are the Lord God who teaches him to profit and leads him in the way he should go, abundantly supplied with every need met! He has obtained the favor of the Lord and the will of God is done in his life!"

SCRIPTURE REFERENCES:

Proverbs 1:33
Proverbs 2:2
Proverbs 3:3
Proverbs 4:8
Proverbs 3:26

Proverbs 6:22
Proverbs 8:6,8
I Peter 3:7-9
Proverbs 11:30
Isaiah 48:17

For a Harmonious Marriage

"Father, in the name of Jesus, it's written in Your Word that love is shed abroad in our hearts by the Holy Ghost who is given to us. Because You are in us, we acknowledge that love reigns supreme. We believe that love is displayed in full expression enfolding and knitting us together in truth, making us perfect for every good work to do Your will, working in us that which is pleasing in Your sight.

"We live and conduct ourselves and our marriage honorably and becomingly. We esteem it as precious, worthy and of great price. **We commit ourselves to live in mutual harmony and accord with one another** delighting in each other, being of the same mind and united in spirit.

"Father, we believe and say that we are gentle, compassionate, courteous, tender-hearted and humble-minded. We seek peace and it keeps our hearts in quietness and assurance. Because we follow after love and dwell in peace, our prayers are not hindered in any way, in the name of Jesus. We are heirs together of the grace of God.

"Our marriage grows stronger day by day in the bond of unity because it is founded on Your Word and rooted and grounded in Your love. Father, we thank You for the performance of it, in Jesus' name."

SCRIPTURE REFERENCES:

Romans 5:5
Philippians 1:9
Colossians 3:14
Colossians 1:10
Philippians 2:13
Philippians 2:2

Ephesians 4:32
Isaiah 32:17
Philippians 4:7
I Peter 3:7
Ephesians 3:17-18
Jeremiah 1:12

For Compatibility in Marriage

"Father, in the name of Jesus, I pray and confess that *(name both names)* endure long and are patient and kind; that we are never envious and never boil over with jealousy. We are not boastful or vainglorious and we do not display ourselves haughtily. _____ are not conceited or arrogant and inflated with pride. We are not rude and unmannerly and we do not act unbecomingly. We do not insist on our own rights or our own way for we are not self-seeking or touchy or fretful or resentful. We take no account of the evil done to us and pay no attention to a suffered wrong. We do not rejoice at injustice and unrighteousness but we rejoice when right and truth prevail.

"We bear up under anything and everything that comes. We are ever ready to believe the best of each other. Our hopes are fadeless under all circumstances. We endure everything without weakening. OUR LOVE NEVER FAILS — it never fades out or becomes obsolete or comes to an end.

"We are confessing that our lives and our family's lives lovingly express truth in all things. That we speak truly, deal truly, and live truly. That we are enfolded in love and have grown up in every way and in all things. We esteem and delight in one another, forgiving one another readily and freely as God in Christ has forgiven us. We are imitators of God and copy His example as well-beloved children imitate their father.

"Thank You, Father, that our marriage grows stronger each day because it is founded on Your Word and on Your kind of love. We give You the praise for it ALL, Father, in the name of Jesus."

SCRIPTURE REFERENCES:

I Corinthians 13:4-8   Ephesians 4:15,32
I Corinthians 14:1   Ephesians 5:1-2

Intercession for a Troubled Marriage

"Father, in the name of Jesus, we bring _____ before You. We pray and confess Your Word over them, and as we do, we use our faith, believing that Your Word will come to pass.

"Therefore we pray and confess that _____ will let all bitterness and indignation and wrath, passion, rage, bad temper and resentment, brawling, clamor, contention and slander, evil speaking, abusive, or blasphemous language be banished from them; also all malice, spite, ill will or baseness of any kind . . . that _____ have become useful and helpful and kind to one another, tenderhearted, compassionate, understanding, lovinghearted, forgiving one another readily and freely as You Father, in Christ, forgave them . . . .

"Therefore, _____ will be imitators of You, God. They will copy You and follow Your example as well-beloved children imitate their father. _____ will walk in love, esteeming and delighting in one another as Christ loved them and gave Himself up for them, a slain offering and sacrifice to You God, so that it became a sweet fragrance."

"SATAN, WE RENDER YOU HELPLESS IN YOUR ACTIVITIES IN _____ LIVES AND COME AGAINST YOU SPIRIT OF SEPARATION AND DIVORCE. WE LOOSE YOU FROM YOUR ASSIGNMENT AGAINST THEM. SATAN, YOUR POWER IS BROKEN FROM THEIR MARRIAGE IN THE NAME OF JESUS."

"Father, we thank You that _____ will be constantly renewed in the spirit of their minds having a fresh mental and spiritual attitude. They have put on the new nature and are created in God's image in true righteousness and holiness. They have come to their senses and escaped out of the snare of the devil that has held them captive and henceforth will do Your will, which is that they love one another with the God kind of love united in total peace and harmony and happiness.

"Thank You for the answer, Lord. We know it is done NOW in the name of Jesus."

SCRIPTURE REFERENCES:

Ephesians 4:31-32   Ephesians 4:23-24
Ephesians 5:1-2   II Timothy 2:26
Matthew 18:18

For Wives

"Father, in the name of Jesus, I take Your Word and speak it out of my mouth and say I have faith that I am a capable, intelligent, patient, and virtuous woman. I am far more precious than jewels. My value to my husband and family is far above rubies and pearls.

"The heart of my husband _____ and my children _____ trusts in me confidently and relies on and believes in me safely, so that they have no lack of honest gain or need of dishonest spoil.

"Father, I will comfort, encourage, and do them only good as long as there is life within me. I gird myself with strength and spiritual, mental, and physical fitness for my God-given task, and I make my arms strong and firm. I taste and see that my gain from work with and for God is good. My lamp goes not out; it burns on continually through the night of any trouble, privation, or sorrow and warns away fear, doubt, and distrust.

"I open my hand to the poor, I reach out my filled hands to the needy — whether in spirit, mind or body. My husband is known as a success in everything he sets his hand to. Strength and dignity are my clothing and my position in my household is strong. I am secure and at peace in knowing as for me and my family we are in readiness for the future. I open my mouth with skillful and godly wisdom and in my tongue is the law of kindness and love. I look well to how things go in my household, and the bread of idleness, gossip, discontent, and self-pity I will not eat.

"My children rise up and call me blessed and happy. My husband boasts of and praises me saying that I excel in all that I set my hand to. I am a woman who reverently and worshipfully loves You, Lord, and You shall give me the fruits of my hands. My works will praise me wherever I go, for Father, I confess that I am a submitted wife — *simply because I want to be.* I thank You for my husband who is head over me, but who has given me (through the chain of command) the necessary power to do what Your Word says for me to do from Proverbs 31:10-31. I am as this woman is — a loving, successful, submitted wife . . . in the name of Jesus.''

SCRIPTURE REFERENCES:

Proverbs 31:10-31

For the 100-fold Return

"Father, in Jesus' name, I give honor to the truth and integrity of Your Word. I thank You for the 100-fold return. I confess before You and all the host of heaven and earth that the 100-fold return is mine. I have given of my life and possessions to follow You. I have given for the Gospel's sake. Now I know the full 100-fold return is working and on its way to me. I confess that You are causing it to come to me in abundance. It belongs to me. *Your Word says it is mine, so I say it is mine.* I have it!

"I receive the abundance of life. I receive Your blessing. It is You who give me the power to get wealth that You may establish Your covenant with me. I thank You that the revelation knowledge of that covenant is steadily increasing in my spirit. The Word of God is true and I know that You are alert and active, watching over Your Word to perform it in my life.

"Father, I am thankful that the blessing of the Lord makes me truly rich and You add no sorrow with it. The loving-kindness and tender mercies of the Lord endure forever. Goodness and mercy are mine all the days of my life in Jesus' name. Amen. So be it!! Praise the Lord!"

SCRIPTURE REFERENCES:

Mark 10:29-30   Jeremiah 1:12
Mark 11:23   Proverbs 10:22
Deuteronomy 8:18   Deuteronomy 30:19
Colossians 1:10   Psalm 23:6

Prosperity for You and Others

"Father, in the name of Your Son, Jesus, we confess Your Word over _____ this day. As we do this, we say it with our mouths and believe it in our hearts and know that Your Word will not return to You void, but will accomplish what it says it will do.

"Therefore, we believe in the name of Jesus that _____ needs are met according to Philippians 4:19. We believe that because _____ has given to further Your cause, Father, gifts will be given to him, good measure, pressed down, shaken together and running over will they pour into his bosom. For with the measure he deals out, it will be measured back to him. Father, we confess a hundredfold return for him according to Mark 10:29-30.

"Father, You have delivered _____ out of the authority of darkness into the kingdom of Your dear Son. Father, we believe _____ has taken his place as Your child. We confess You have assumed Your place as his Father and have made Your home with _____ . You are taking care of him and even now enabling him to walk in love and in wisdom, and to walk in the fullness of fellowship with Your Son."

"SATAN, WE BIND YOU FROM _____ FINANCES ACCORDING TO MATTHEW 18:18 AND LOOSE YOU FROM YOUR ASSIGNMENT AGAINST HIM."

"We thank You, that the ministering spirits which You have given to him are now free to minister for _____ and bring in the necessary finances.

"Father, we confess You are a very present help in trouble, and You are more than enough. We confess, God, You are able to make all grace, every favor and earthly blessing, come to

_____ in abundance, so that he is always and in all circumstances and whatever the need, self-sufficient, possessing enough to require no aid or support and furnished in abundance for every good work and charitable donation.''

SCRIPTURE REFERENCES:

Isaiah 55:11

Philippians 4:19

Luke 6:38

Mark 10:29,30

Colossians 1:13

II Corinthians 6:16,18

Matthew 18:18

Hebrews 1:14

II Corinthians 9:8

Psalm 46:1

A Dedication for Your Tithes

"We profess this day unto the Lord God that we have come into the inheritance which the Lord swore to give us. We are in the land which You have provided for us in Jesus Christ, the kingdom of almighty God. We were sinners serving Satan, he was our god. But we called upon the name of Jesus and You heard our cry and delivered us into the kingdom of Your dear Son.

"Jesus, as our Lord and High Priest, we bring the first fruits of our income to You and worship the Lord our God with it.

"We rejoice in all the good which You have given to us and our household. We have hearkened to the voice of the Lord our God and have done according to all that He has commanded us. Now look down from your holy habitation from heaven and bless us as You said in Your Word. We thank You, Father, in Jesus' name."

SCRIPTURE REFERENCES:

Deuteronomy 26:1,3,10,11,14,15 Colossians 1:13
Ephesians 2:1-5   Hebrews 3:1,7-8

References

1. Adams, Billie, "Dynamic Prayer Power" (tapes)

2. Capps, Charles, "Prayer that Changes Things" (tape)

3. Copeland, Gloria, *God's Will for You*

4. Copeland, Kenneth, *Believer's Voice of Victory* (newsletters) and *"God's Plan for Your Life"* (tract)

5. Hagin, Kenneth, *Man on Three Dimensions* and *Praying to Get Results* and *Faith Food* (summer)

6. Kenyon, E. W., *In His Presence*

You may contact Word Ministries by writing:

Word Ministries, Inc.
P.O. Box 76532
Atlanta, GA 30358

*Feel free to include your prayer requests and comments
when you write.*

Prayers That Avail Much
is available at your local bookstore.

HARRISON HOUSE
P. O. Box 35035 • Tulsa, OK 74153